Train Your Dog ...In No Time

H. Ellen Whiteley, D.V.M.

 800 East 96th Street
Indianapolis, Indiana 46240

Train Your Dog In No Time

Copyright © 2006 by H. Ellen Whiteley, D.V.M.

All rights reserved. No part of this book shall be reproduced, stored in a retrieval system, or transmitted by any means, electronic, mechanical, photocopying, recording, or otherwise, without written permission from the publisher. No patent liability is assumed with respect to the use of the information contained herein. Although every precaution has been taken in the preparation of this book, the publisher and author assume no responsibility for errors or omissions. Nor is any liability assumed for damages resulting from the use of the information contained herein.

International Standard Book Number: 0-7897-3225-4

Library of Congress Catalog Card Number: 2005928026

Printed in the United States of America

First Printing: October 2005

08 07 06 05   4 3 2 1

Trademarks

All terms mentioned in this book that are known to be trademarks or service marks have been appropriately capitalized. Que Publishing cannot attest to the accuracy of this information. Use of a term in this book should not be regarded as affecting the validity of any trademark or service mark.

Warning and Disclaimer

Every effort has been made to make this book as complete and as accurate as possible, but no warranty or fitness is implied. The information provided is on an "as is" basis. The author and the publisher shall have neither liability nor responsibility to any person or entity with respect to any loss or damages arising from the information contained in this book.

Bulk Sales

Que Publishing offers excellent discounts on this book when ordered in quantity for bulk purchases or special sales. For more information, please contact

U.S. Corporate and Government Sales
1-800-382-3419
corpsales@pearsontechgroup.com

For sales outside of the U.S., please contact

International Sales
international@pearsoned.com

Executive Editors
Rick Kughen
Candace Hall

Development Editor
Lorna Gentry

Managing Editor
Charlotte Clapp

Project Editor
Dan Knott

Copy Editor
Rhonda Tinch-Mize

Indexer
Erika Millen

Proofreader
Elizabeth Scott

Technical Editor
Jamie Young

Publishing Coordinator
Cindy Teeters

Book Designer
Ann Jones

Page Layout
TnT Design
Toi Davis

Graphics
Stephen Adams

Contents at a Glance

Introduction 1

Part I First Things First 7
1 What You Should Know About Your Dog 9
2 What You Should Know About Training 27
3 Getting Ready for Training 37

Part II Train Your Dog or Puppy In No Time 47
4 Manners Training: Week by Week 49
5 Graduating to Next-Level Basics 71
6 Having Fun with Simple Tricks 85
7 Having Fun While Exercising 93

Part III Improving Your Dog's Manners 103
8 Housetraining in Every Way 105
9 Eliminating Annoying Habits 117
10 Getting Tough About Serious Offenses 127

Part IV Appendixes 143
A References and Resources 145
B Planning Charts 153
Index 161

Table of Contents

Introduction 1

Who Should Read This Book 3

How This Book Is Organized 4
    The Book's Parts 4
    Special Icons 5

Everyone Wins 6

I First Things First

1 What You Should Know About Your Dog 9

Understanding Your Dog's Personality 10
    Influences of Age 11
    Influences of Gender 11
    Breed Considerations 12

Assessing Your Dog's Temperament 12
    Explore Your Puppy or Dog's Temperament 13

Setting the Stage: Critical Periods of Development 14
    Socializing Your Puppy 15
    Socializing Your Adolescent Dog 20
    Socializing an Older Dog 20

Making Introductions 21
    Preparing Your Dog for Baby 22
    Introducing a New Dog to Your Children and Other Family Members . 23
    Introducing a New Puppy or Dog to Your Current Pet 23

Summary 26

2 What You Should Know About Training 27

Determining Your Dog's Aptitudes and Training Needs 28
    Your Dog's Aptitude for Learning 28
    Using Body Language to Discern Your Dog's Training Needs 28

Integrating Training Methods into Family Life 30
    Selecting a Head Trainer 31
    Where to Train 31
    When to Train 32

Learning the Rules of Training 33
    Sending a Clear Message 33

  Giving Immediate Feedback 34
  Making Training Fair and Fun 35

 Summary 35

3 Getting Ready for Training 37

 Preparing Your Dog's Spaces 38
  Choosing and Locating the Crate 38
  Choosing and Locating the Dog House 40
  Preparing for Yard, Paper, or Litter Box Training 40

 Buying Equipment and Supplies 42
  Choosing a Collar and Leash 43
  Selecting Treats 43
  What You Should Know About Toys 45
  Selecting Cleaning Products for Training Accidents 46

 Summary 46

II Train Your Dog or Puppy In No Time

4 Manners Training: Week by Week 49

 Week One: Using Commands and Beginning Basic Crate and
  House Training 50
  Choosing and Using Commands 50
  Crate Training 51
  Toilet Training 53

 Week Two: Adding Basic Commands and Stopping Unwanted Behaviors . 56
  Teaching Your Dog to Come When Called 57
  Teaching "Sit" 57
  Preventing Unwanted Puppy Chewing 60
  Curbing Puppy Biting Behavior 60

 Week Three: Introducing Leash Walking 62
  Leash Walking Basics 62
  Teaching Your Dog to Turn with You 63

 Week Four: Adding the Down Command 64

 Week Five: Introducing "Stay" and the Release Word 66

 Week Six: Teaching Your Dog to Remain in the "Down" Position .. 68
  Teaching the "Down-Stay" 68
  Having Patience with Your Pet 69

 Summary 69

5 Graduating to Next-Level Basics 71

Continuing with Recall and Leash Training 71
    Another Technique for Teaching "Come" 72
    Teaching the "Heel" Command 74

Teaching Hand Signals 75
    Getting Your Dog's Attention by Clapping ... 77
    Using Hand Signals for Heel, Come, Sit, Down,
    and Stay 78

Introducing Clickers and Other Event Markers 80
    Using a Clicker 81
    Using the Clicker to Introduce Nail Trimming 81

Summary 83

6 Having Fun with Simple Tricks 85

Teaching Your Dog Tricks 86
    Considering the Benefits of Trick Training 86
    Choosing the Right Tricks for Your Dog 86

Training for Bell Ringing 87

Selecting Fun Tricks 89
    Teaching Roll Over 89
    Wowing with Bowing 90
    Jumping Through Hoops 91
    Teaching "Play Dead" 92

Summary 92

7 Having Fun While Exercising 93

Making Exercise Part of Your Dog's Routine 94
    Choosing the Right Exercise for Your Dog 95
    Conditioning for Exercise 95

Hiking and Backpacking 96
    Choosing Doggy Packs and Other Supplies 97
    Following Trail Etiquette 98

Introducing Water Sports 99
    Teaching Your Dog to Swim 99
    Considering Life Jackets 100

Playing Fetch 101
    Teaching Your Dog to Fetch 101

Considering Athletic Competitions 102

Summary 102

III Improving Your Dog's Manners

8 Housetraining in Every Way 105

Discouraging Potty Accidents 105
   Tracking Down and Treating the Cause 106
   Retraining 107
   Curbing Submissive and Excitement-Induced Urination 108
   Putting an End to Marking Behavior 109

Teaching Your Dog Home and Garden Rules 109
   Keeping Your Dog Off the Furniture 110
   Putting an End to Stealing 112
   Ending the Yard Excavations 112

Cleaning Up Your Dog's Eating and Drinking Habits 114
   Ceasing to Reward Begging 114
   Preventing Toilet Drinking 115
   Closing the Poop Buffet 116

Summary 116

9 Eliminating Annoying Habits 117

Silencing Excessive Vocalizations 117
   Dealing with Excessive Barking, Howling, or Whining 118
   Correcting with Distraction and Punishment 120

Putting a Stop to Jumping Up 121
   Making Corrections 121

Putting a Stop to Gate and Door Rushing . . 123
   Ending Pushy Behavior at Doors
   and Gates 123
   Teaching Proper Doorbell Etiquette 124

What to Do When Your Dog Gets Personal . 125
   Ending Nose-to-Crotch Sniffing 126
   Putting an End to Mounting 126

Summary 126

10 Getting Tough About Serious Offenses 127

Putting a Stop to Aggression 127
    Incorporating Tough Love for the Dominant Pooch 130
    Preventing Fear Biting 132
    Correcting Territorial Aggression 133

Controlling Predatory Behavior 134
    Preventing Predatory Behavior Toward Animals or People 135
    Curbing the Car Chaser 137

Reducing the Anxiety of Separation 137
    Reading the Clues 138
    Treating Separation Anxiety 138

Reducing Your Dog's Fearful Reactions 140
    Calming the Scared Dog 141

Summary 142

IV Appendices

A References and Resources 145

Selecting a Dog 145
    Choosing the Ideal Dog: A Questionnaire 146
    Accommodating Allergic Family Members 146
    Accommodating Young Children 146
    Where to Find a Dog 147

Selecting a Trainer, Behavioral Consultant, or Veterinary Behaviorist .. 149
    Selecting an Obedience Instructor or Dog Trainer 149
    Selecting a Behavioral Consultant or Veterinary Behaviorist 150

Useful Websites, Telephone Numbers, and Books 150
    Information 150
    Products 151
    Books 152

B Planning Charts 153

Daily Toilet Training Diary 154

Weekly Obedience Training Logs 155
    Weekly Obedience Training Log: "Come" and "Sit" (Introduced
    Week 2, Chapter 4) 155
    Weekly Obedience Training Log: "Walk" (Introduced Week 3,
    Chapter 4) 156

Weekly Obedience Training Log: "Down" (Introduced Week 4, Chapter 4) 157
Weekly Obedience Training Log: "Sit-Stay" (Introduced Week 5, Chapter 4) 158
Weekly Obedience Training Log: "Down-Stay" (Introduced Week 6, Chapter 4) 159

Index 161

About the Author

H. Ellen Whiteley, D.V.M., is an internationally published and award-winning author. Her books include *Women In Veterinary Medicine: Profiles of Success*, ISU Press, 1991; *Understanding and Training Your Cat or Kitten*, Crown, 1994; and *Understanding and Training Your Dog or Puppy*, Crown, 1996. The last two titles were translated into Russian. As a columnist for professional and consumer magazines, her byline has appeared in *The Saturday Evening Post*, *Woman's World Magazine*, *Milwaukee Sentinel*, and others.

As a veterinarian, Dr. Whiteley has worked in diverse jobs: She has served as a military veterinarian, a national rabies awareness spokesperson, a poultry inspector, an instructor of veterinary technology, and a practicing veterinarian.

An avid hiker, Whiteley trekked in Nepal and climbed Africa's Kilimanjaro. She lives in the Sangre de Cristo Mountains of New Mexico with her husband George. For more information about the author, her books, articles about pet care, and a potty store for dogs and cats, visit her website at www.drwhiteley.com.

Dedication

To my canine patients and to the memory of Bear and to all the dogs that taught and continue to teach me about canine behavior and training. And to my human family who are with me in all of life's adventures.

Acknowledgments

I appreciate the assistance and technical guidance of the entire staff at Que. Special thanks to Candace Hall who brought me onboard for this project and Lorna Gentry, editor extraordinaire. Thanks also to girlfriends Beverly and Andi, who share their support and their dogs with me on a daily basis.

We Want to Hear from You!

As the reader of this book, *you* are our most important critic and commentator. We value your opinion and want to know what we're doing right, what we could do better, what areas you'd like to see us publish in, and any other words of wisdom you're willing to pass our way.

As an executive editor for Que Publishing, I welcome your comments. You can email or write me directly to let me know what you did or didn't like about this book—as well as what we can do to make our books better.

Please note that I cannot help you with technical problems related to the topic of this book. We do have a User Services group, however, where I will forward specific technical questions related to the book.

When you write, please be sure to include this book's title and author as well as your name, email address, and phone number. I will carefully review your comments and share them with the author and editors who worked on the book.

Email: feedback@quepublishing.com

Mail: Rick Kughen
Executive Editor
Que Publishing
800 East 96th Street
Indianapolis, IN 46240 USA

For more information about this book or another Que Publishing title, visit our website at www.quepublishing.com. Type the ISBN (excluding hyphens) or the title of a book in the Search field to find the page you're looking for.

Introduction

Most of us start out with a picture of life that includes marriage to Prince (or Princess) Charming, children who grow up to be Bill Gates, and a dog like Lassie. My client Melissa Delaney's family dream was starting to come together. She lived congenially with a five-year old Schnauzer with many Lassie-like qualities and was engaged to marry a man who was her Prince Charming.

Unfortunately, the honeymoon period ended too quickly. Melissa called my office one day with a crisis. Gretchen, the Schnauzer, hated the new husband, and refused to let him enter Melissa's bedroom. The frustrated husband had issued an ultimatum: "Either that dog goes, or I go!"

A significant number of crises occurring in veterinary hospitals and at home involve canine behavioral issues much like Melissa was describing. Gretchen, who had previously shared her mistress's bed and sole affection, viewed Mr. Delaney not as Prince Charming but as the Hulk, someone to be banished from the formerly peaceful kingdom.

Many disasters such as this one can be averted by socializing your dog and teaching him basic obedience commands as soon as he becomes a family member. If Gretchen had been introduced to men during puppyhood, she would have accepted the husband more readily. If she had been taught basic obedience commands at a young age, peace at home could have been more readily reinstated. Was it too late for the newlyweds? Of course not. Mature dogs can be conditioned to accept new people and situations, and they can learn obedience commands. Still, socializing and teaching proper conduct early in your relationship means that canine training proceeds more efficiently and quickly.

Training your dog efficiently and quickly is what this book is about. The *"In No Time"* series caters to busy people—often juggling family, career, and community obligations—who have added "training the dog" to their hectic schedules. Few of you have time to peruse an extensive tome offering elaborate details about behavioral theory and training methods. *Train Your Dog In No Time*, instead, offers concise, organized, and easy-to-do instruction. Its step by step approach shows you how to train or retrain your dog with minimal time and hassle. Having a well-trained dog saves time in the long run. In Chapter 1, "What You Should Know About Your Dog," you learn more about Gretchen the Schnauzer and how to introduce family members and others to your dog in a nonthreatening way.

Here are just some of the things you'll learn in this book:

- The factors such as breed and gender that shape your dog's personality
- Ways to socialize your puppy or dog to accept new people and situations
- The training methods that work with your dog and those that don't
- How to organize the "spaces" where your dog lives
- Suggestions for training supplies
- The techniques for teaching the basic commands—come, sit, down, stay, and heel
- Ideas for exercising with and teaching tricks to your pet
- How to incorporate hand signals, obedience classes, and clickers into your training regime
- How to retrain the dog that is disobeying house rules—having accidents in the house or jumping on the furniture, for example
- Corrections for annoying habits such as door rushing and crotch sniffing
- The factors that influence serious misbehavior such as aggression to people or other animals and who to call for help

INTRODUCTION

Who Should Read This Book

This book is written and designed to work for you regardless of where you fall in the dog-owning continuum: pre-adoption, recently acquired a puppy or dog, or long-standing relationship with the family canine/canines. In the latter case, you may elect to skip certain sections. However, reading the chapters pertaining primarily to puppies may reveal to you the reasons that your adult dog is misbehaving. We—people and dogs—are products of our upbringing and early conditioning.

In other words, just about anyone who is interested in the benefits of having a well-trained dog should read this book. Perhaps you fit in one of the following scenarios:

- You are planning to adopt a puppy or adult dog. This book presents information about gender, age, and breed characteristics which help you with that decision. If you already own a dog, you will learn the factors influencing his personality and trainability.

- You have postponed your dog's training but now realize the timesaving benefits of spending a few minutes each day training your dog to be a companionable family member. Learn from this book what you need to get started immediately.

- Your dog is experiencing a breakdown in training and must be retrained to correct an existing behavioral problem or problems. Read this book for proven correction methods.

- Your home situation is changing—you are moving to a new home, having a baby, getting married, inviting the grandparents to stay for the summer—and you need to know what you can do to lessen your dog's stress and to condition him to new circumstances.

- You realize that training your dog to properly walk on a leash and obey basic commands are essential to his safety when visiting the park or traveling in the car.

- You know that training can mean the difference between your dog becoming a nuisance or a companionable friend.

- You want to have fun and impress the kids by teaching your dog tricks. Perhaps your dog is bored—a prime motivator for getting into trouble. Teaching your dog tricks is a positive way to alleviate boredom and to bond with your pet.

- You realize the many health benefits of exercising with your dog. My personal exercise program includes trekking with friends and a variety of dogs and llamas. Read this book to learn trail etiquette and the benefits of teaching your dog to carry a pack containing his food and your heavy water bottle.

- Your child is training his dog as a 4H or school project, and you want a handy, concise reference on the subject.

How This Book Is Organized

Fitting dog training into your busy schedule might seem a daunting task. As mentioned previously, however, not training your dog is more costly in terms of time and trouble than spending a few minutes a day in focused training sessions teaching your dog to be a good canine citizen.

I suggest that you examine the extensive Table of Contents and scan the book in its entirety to get a feel for the information and how it's presented. When applicable, chapters offer a "To do list" and "You'll need list." These lists help you identify the training lessons covered in that chapter, as well as the tools or supplies that you need to buy or have on hand. Most people then elect to proceed sequentially through the book. All lessons build upon those that precede them. So, for example, after you've learned the basic "words" you will use to communicate with your canine friend, you know the correct language to use in subsequent training sessions. You can always move to later chapters as necessary, however; if your dog has acceptable house manners, and you are reading the book to rectify annoying outdoor habits such as digging in the flower beds or chasing cars, feel free to proceed directly to the appropriate section and begin correcting those bad habits.

The Book's Parts

Train Your Dog In No Time is organized in such a way that you can absorb its information in small bites of time scrounged from your lunch break and car pool duties. The book is divided into 10 chapters, and the chapters fall logically into three major parts:

- In Part I, "First Things First," you'll learn the factors that shape your dog's personality. These include breed, age, gender, and early socialization. Part I outlines the rules of training and how to prepare for the training sessions that are to follow. You will learn how to choose and locate your dog's crate; how to select and prepare for toilet training using paper, canine litter box, or outdoor methods; and what training aids to buy or have on hand.

- In Part II, "Train Your Dog or Puppy In No Time," we get to the real nitty-gritty of training. You'll learn how to proceed with crate and toilet training, how to select your puppy's name, and how to use verbal commands to communicate with your dog. After you have introduced your dog to the crate (his home within your home) and to his bathroom, we proceed with weekly lessons to learn walking on a loose leash and the basic obedience commands of sit, come, down, and stay. You may elect to pause here, or you may be having so much fun that you want to take training to the next level by partaking of subsequent instructions for heeling; using clickers and teaching hand signals. In Part II, I make suggestions for teaching your dog tricks and/or exercising with your dog. Although tricks and exercise are the final chapters in this part, you may choose to introduce them earlier in order to complete a day's training session on a positive note by playing a game of fetch or swimming with your dog.

- In Part III, "Improving Your Dog's Manners," I offer retraining methods for potty accidents; corrections for breaking house rules by jumping on the furniture, begging, and more; and suggestions for breaking your dog of annoying personal habits such as barking or jumping up on people. Chapter 10, the last chapter, is devoted to more serious offenses such as aggression toward people and other animals, separation anxiety, and phobias. Some of these behaviors can be difficult to control and might prove, in the case of an aggressive dog, for instance, to be dangerous to you, others, or your property. Part of being a savvy owner is knowing when to seek help. I'll make suggestions about who to consult when you need professional help with a serious canine behavioral problem.

- Part IV, "Appendixes," gives you resources for choosing a dog and selecting professional assistance, as well as a list of references of useful websites and telephone numbers. Appendix B offers some useful training logs and charts to help you track your dog's progress.

Special Icons

Train Your Dog In No Time is designed to help you absorb its information quickly and effectively. Each chapter starts with a succinct introduction and an eye-catching list of the major topics you'll learn about within the chapter. In addition to the "To do" and "You'll need" lists mentioned earlier, chapter text is interspersed with notes, tips, cautions, and sidebars that offer interesting information that supplement the regular chapter text and expand your understanding of the related topic. Each chapter ends with a brief summary reiterating what you have accomplished to this point in your training program.

As you read through the book, you'll also notice a number of graphic icons in the margins. These small pictures are used to alert you to important text that falls into specific categories:

Material marked with the Dog Speak icon describes what your dog is telling you with his body language, vocalizations, and/or facial expressions.

The Training Tip icon alerts you to information containing professional advice for specific training situations or canine personalities.

 The Old Dog Tales icon tells you that an old myth about dogs or their training is being refuted with updated information.

 Fetch alerts you to text or sidebars containing product or resource information.

 Repeat Performance reminds you that this material was presented earlier and bears mentioning again in the present context.

Everyone Wins

All dogs benefit from training, and I commend you on your decisions to buy this book and to start teaching your dog proper manners and good canine citizenship. A well-mannered dog is a pleasure to spend time with and to have as a family member. As my hero James Herriot says, "A dog likes to obey. It gives them security."

Part 1

First Things First

1 What You Should Know About Your Dog .. 9

2 What You Should Know About Training .. 27

3 Getting Ready for Training 37

What You Should Know About Your Dog

In this chapter:

* Learn the factors that influence your dog's personality and behavior
* Learn critical periods for teaching and socializing your dog
* Make the introductions and prepare your resident dog to accept your new baby or an adopted dog or cat

What kind of dog is ideal for you? A small, friendly breed that will fit into your efficiency apartment? A rambunctious dog that can hold his own in your family of five adolescent boys? A watch dog for your country estate? A sedate, laid-back dog to provide companionship for your elderly mother? A dog just like the one killed in an accident when you were 12 years old? Everyone will answer this question differently.

Some of you, I'm sure, will reply that your dog found you, and not the other way around. Your dog is the one the neighbors abandoned when they moved to Fiji or the one your teenage daughter left permanently at your house when she departed for a distant college. In these cases, you take what you've got and try to mold the fellow into the ideal dog for you.

In this chapter, we'll look at some of the factors influencing canine personality or behavior. The information you learn here will help you understand the background influences shaping your dog's personality. These influences include breed, age, gender, and early socialization. Socialization is, quite simply, the act of teaching your dog to be social and well adjusted to the world he lives in. Regardless of whether your dog is young or old,

I'll lead you through this process. And, we'll discuss the steps you can take with your puppy to help ensure that he grows up to be a more resilient adult, less vulnerable to the stress that change evokes in many of us, canine or human.

To do list

- ❏ Understand the relationship between a dog's age and behavior
- ❏ Learn how gender influences a dog's behavior and learn the attributes of males and females
- ❏ Become familiar with the physical and personality traits of your dog's breed

Understanding Your Dog's Personality

The contrast in physical traits within the dog world is phenomenal. As illustrated in Figure 1.1, dogs vary greatly in physical attributes; a tiny, smooth-haired Chihuahua falls in the same species as a giant, hairy Saint Bernard. Breed type and upbringing, rather than size and physical attributes, determine a dog's personality.

FIGURE 1.1
Dogs offer great diversity in physical appearance and personality.

CHAPTER 1   What You Should Know About Your Dog

Like us, an individual dog's early family history has a tremendous impact on determining character traits. Is he an orphan? A shelter dog? Is he young, old, female or male, neutered or intact? Was he raised with dogs, people, or other animals? These questions can be further subdivided into what kind of dogs live with you presently and how many; which people—babies, children, grandparents—and what animals—cats, mice, horses, llamas? We'll explore these questions and more in the following sections.

Influences of Age

Puppies are almost irresistible. They are one of the true "warm fuzzies" in life. However, their angelic appearance can soon be overshadowed by the realities of their precocious and energetic antics. A puppy requires more attention than an adult dog. He needs to eat at least three times a day and requires frequent supervised trips to the potty. During the teething stage, he might attempt to eat your back door or gnaw your furniture. (If you are a puppy owner saying, "Yeah, that sounds familiar," go directly to "Preventing Puppy Chewing" in Chapter 4, "Manners Training: Week by Week," to immediately put a stop to this behavior.)

In some ways, puppies are pure potential, at least behaviorally. With a puppy, you have the opportunity to shape his personality. But, if your job and community obligations require you to stay away from home most of the day, you might want to consider adopting an adult.

Don't fall for the common wisdom that you need to get a puppy in order to really bond with and thoroughly train your dog. Using the techniques you learn in this book, you can train dogs of *any* age. Although adult dogs are already formed in appearance and habits, they are trainable and they may have outgrown some of the more time-consuming and destructive habits of puppies. An adult dog's good habits are an asset, and with time and patience you can undo bad habits.

Influences of Gender

The bestseller, *Men are from Mars, Women are from Venus*, had us discussing male/female differences in the human sexes. Dogs have gender differences, too. For instance, females typically are easier to housebreak and train than males. Males usually require more time for play and exercise than females and are more likely to urinate around the yard or house to mark their territory.

Neutering eliminates most unwanted sexual conduct such as sexually motivated roaming and mating behavior, but neutering does not make a dog calmer, less destructive, or less aggressive toward people. In breeds known for high aggression and/or an excitable nature, females typically (but not always) tend to be less aggressive and calmer than males. In case it sounds as if I am categorically recommending females, I should add a disclaimer. My favorite personal dogs have all been male; albeit they were by nature laid-back and yes, in the case of Bear, somewhat difficult to train.

Breed Considerations

Your dog or puppy's physical and personality traits are influenced by his mother and father. If both parents are the same breed, the genes that determine certain behavior are more concentrated. If you have a purebred Labrador Retriever, for instance, you can expect by nature of his ancestry that he will be easily

> **tip** If you are considering adopting a new dog, see "Selecting a Dog" in Appendix A, "References and Resources." There, you'll find helpful information to assist you in making this important decision.

trained to respond to obedience commands and will perhaps, if you are persistent and patient in your training, learn to open the lid to the cooler and bring you a cold Budweiser. He is not going to be overly demanding of affection and will generally be a quiet and loving pet. However, if you expect him to guard your home like a Doberman Pinscher, you are probably going to be disappointed.

What happens if your pet is a crossbreed with a purebred Doberman for one parent and a Lab for the other? You can expect a blending of personality traits, gaining, with proper training, a pet that will bring you a beer and guard the backyard. Mixed breed dogs fall in a slightly different category; you can't predict their temperament or adult size based on breed characteristics. These mongrels have unknown parentage and are commonly called a "Heinz" because of all the ingredients composing their lineages. Many great dogs fall into this category.

The American Kennel Club (AKC) at (919-233-9767) or www.akc.org offers detailed information about the 150 breeds in its registry. This information includes size, temperament, grooming needs, and general care. The AKC website provides links to the national breed club for each of these breeds; breed club sites often provide information about prevalent genetic problems and tests for their detection.

To do list

- ❏ Use some simple tests to reveal your puppy's temperament
- ❏ Prepare to accommodate your dog's potential and needs during training

Assessing Your Dog's Temperament

Many factors go into making your dog a "good fit" for your household, and training is one of the most important ones. Your home situation, the ages, experience, and occupations of the people who live there, and the amount of time and money you can devote to your pet all determine how you can go about training your dog to fit well within your household.

CHAPTER 1   What You Should Know About Your Dog

Things You'll Need

- ❑ Your dog or puppy
- ❑ Puppy Aptitude Test
- ❑ Computer and online access

Explore Your Puppy or Dog's Temperament

If you've just brought your new puppy or dog into the household, one of your first tasks might be to determine exactly what kinds of personality traits he's exhibiting. You can use that assessment to help target the types of behavior changes you want to focus on in your training.

Temperament tests are designed to give you a clue about the personality traits of individual puppies within a litter. Basically, you are trying to discover if specific puppies are fearful, aggressive, submissive, playful, and so on. Even if you've already adopted a new puppy or a full-grown dog, this kind of testing can help you highlight and understand the kind of temperament your dog is exhibiting.

To begin, walk quietly into the room and sit down near the dog or puppy. Offer your hand, palm turned up, and give a short welcoming salutation—"Hi, guy," or something like that. Does the dog approach you with curiosity? Does he run to the corner and try to hide? Does he snap at your pants legs? Clap your hands to see if the dog approaches you. Walk away and see if he follows. Throw a ball and see what happens. Does the dog shy away, or does he go over to look at it or nudge it with his paw or nose? Puppies and dogs who show a friendly interest in both you and the ball typically are easier to train than those that seem fearful and reserved.

> **tip** If you are adopting from a breeder who is knowledgeable about puppy temperament testing, ask for his assistance in administering and interpreting test results. An experienced breeder is a good resource for recommending the pup most suitable for your family.

Pick up a puppy (or adult dog of manageable size) and cradle him on his back in one arm while placing the other hand gently on his chest. For large dogs, gently roll him onto his spine while crouching on the floor over him. If the dog is a dominant personality, he will struggle, twist, and try to bite you. If fearful, he might act panic-stricken, be stiff, or show other signs of fear such as crying and whining. A submissive dog will be

> **caution** Temperament tests are not fail-safe methods of choosing your lifelong friend, especially if you are a stranger or the mother or litter are stressed by the extra noise and confusion of children and other visitors. So, take it as one more tool to combine with other factors discussed in this chapter.

subdued or cowed. A friendly, confident dog might initially struggle, but will soon relax in response to encouraging words.

Jack and Wendy Volhard, canine obedience instructors and authors, developed a comprehensive Puppy Aptitude Test. This test, designed primarily for puppies around seven weeks of age, enables you to score a pup according to his reaction in 11 categories, such as social dominance and social attraction. A printable version of the test and a table for an interpretation of the scores are found at http://siriusdog.com/articles/volhard-puppy-aptitude-test.htm.

To do list

- Introduce your puppy to new experiences and guide him through fears, phobias, and first visits to the vet
- Give your adolescent dog a socialization refresher course
- Retrain your adult dog for acceptable social behavior

Setting the Stage: Critical Periods of Development

Socialization is the process whereby a puppy develops an identity as a dog and bonds with his own species, other animals, and humans. Puppies begin this process around three to four weeks of age. By this time, the canine babies are exerting their independence, and the canine mother encourages self-sufficiency by avoiding or snapping at those intent upon nursing. Weaning takes place, and play and exploratory behavior with littermates occupy much of a pup's day. Soon, individual pups are adopted by their new families. This takes place ideally between seven and eight weeks of age.

As Table 1.1 illustrates, the critical stages of a puppy's development continue until 8 months of age or even later.

CHAPTER 1   What You Should Know About Your Dog   15

Table 1.1   Critical Periods of Social Development

Social Learning	Critical Age
Socialization to other dogs	Weeks 3 to 8
Socialization to other animals	Weeks 3 to 12
Socialization to people	Weeks 5 and 7 to 12
Adaptation to novel experiences	Weeks 5 and 12 to 16
Fear imprinting	Weeks 7 to 14
2nd fear imprinting period	Months 6 to 14
Leadership classification period	Weeks 12 to 16
Flight instinct period	Months 4 to 8

In this section of the chapter, you learn the important ways a puppy continues to grow and develop throughout these critical stages.

Things You'll Need

- ❏ Your dog
- ❏ Dog treats
- ❏ Puppy toys
- ❏ Bag to use as "diaper bag"
- ❏ Puppy blanket
- ❏ Paper towels and cleaning solution

Socializing Your Puppy

The period between three and four weeks of age and continuing to around twelve weeks of age is the most impressionable time of a puppy's life. Social learning takes place rapidly and easily during this time. Bad habits learned during this stage imprint upon the puppy's mind and might be difficult to change at a later date. The most critical window for socializing your puppy during this two-month period occurs when he is six to eight weeks of age, the age when most puppies go to a new home.

caution Isolated puppies tend to become attached to their physical environment and the objects it contains, experiencing distress when removed from a familiar setting. These individuals are vulnerable to developing separation anxiety when left alone. Further, puppies who aren't exposed to people of varying body size, age, and gender might be fearful when confronting people unlike those they are accustomed to.

Puppies staying with breeders for extended periods (up to three to four months of age) often fear new places and situations. These pups become extremely fearful or timid when exposed to walking in the park, traveling in the car, or any event they failed to experience when they were in that critical period between three and four months of age. For all these reasons, it is important to query breeders in detail about puppy's first months.

First Days at Home

At about eight weeks of age, pups develop preferences for specific kinds of potty locations and surfaces, such as grass or newspaper. A puppy kept for prolonged periods in a kennel or pet store might have already developed these inclinations by the time you adopt him and thus be more challenging to toilet train if you choose a different system. In general, changing your dog's toilet habits isn't an insurmountable problem, but it requires gradually training your dog to switch to new surfaces or locations.

> **note** Every puppy is an individual and might develop earlier or later than his peers in specific areas of socialization. In general, smaller dogs tend to experience these periods earlier than large dogs.

After bringing your puppy home, give him a few days to adjust to household members and his surroundings (see "Making Introductions," later in this chapter). Make sure to familiarize your dog to as many different kinds of people as possible, including elderly people, children, loud teenagers, or people in uniform, as shown in Figure 1.2.

When visitors come to your home, give them toys and treats to offer the puppy; supply the mailman with puppy treats, too. Ask the person to calmly offer the treat to the puppy, and then let the puppy approach; respond with ample praise when the puppy accepts the gift. If the puppy acts fearful, don't force him. Ask the visitor to toss treats from a distance until the puppy gains confidence. The visit need not be long, but should proceed in a welcoming way so that the puppy knows that you hold the visitor in high regard.

The puppy should also become familiar with the things and experiences that will play a role in his future life with you. Introduce him to as many people, animals, places, and events as you possibly can to help your puppy become comfortable with his world and confident that new experiences don't necessarily represent danger.

Fears, Phobias, and First Visits to the Vet

Fear imprints readily in puppies from age seven to fourteen weeks. If the dog is frightened or traumatized during an experience within this critical phase of development, a fear of the people, places, and events involved will remain *imprinted* in the dog's memory; alleviating that fear will require much work and training. This period overlaps the time the pup is introduced to his new home and caretakers, trips in the car, and visits to the veterinarian, so you must be very careful that such experiences are positive for the puppy.

Pack a "puppy diaper bag" for trips in the car and visits to the vet or groomer. Include edible treats, small toys, your pup's favorite blanket (one with a familiar and comforting scent), and a few cleanup items such as paper towels and a small bottle of Urine-Off (discussed in more depth in Chapter 3, "Getting Ready for Training").

CHAPTER 1   What You Should Know About Your Dog   **17**

FIGURE 1.2
Introducing your puppy to many ages and types of people will help him become social and friendly toward strangers and future members of your household.

Ask your veterinarian's staff to schedule a couple of socialization visits to the office prior to your pup's first "real" visit as a patient. During the socialization appointment, your pet is introduced to the waiting and exam rooms. Encourage staff members to pet the puppy, offer him a treat, and perhaps place him on the exam table for a minute or two of praise and soft touching, as shown in Figure 1.3. This procedure can help alleviate veterinary office stress for older dogs, too, but usually less effectively than with impressionable youngsters.

tip   Because disease transmission is a concern for young puppies, ask to schedule an early morning visit before the waiting room is filled with sick patients.

Noise phobias are common in dogs, and many develop during the fear-imprinting stage in a puppy's life. Sometimes, the fear is a general one, and the dog shies away and becomes apprehensive to any loud nose. In other cases, the fear is specific to certain noises such as firecrackers, gunshots, or thunder. It makes sense to avoid exposing your puppy to these loud noises if possible during the fear-imprinting stage. If avoidance is not possible, divert his attention with play or other activity.

Puppy Classes

Many area trainers and veterinarians offer socialization classes for puppies between the ages of two to four months old. (You should be able to restrain your pup with a leash before joining the class.)

The purpose of classes is to get your puppy together with other pups—of differing sizes, breeds, and temperaments—and their owners. Under the guidance of the class instructor, you will learn to introduce your pup to other dogs and to a variety of people, and you will teach your dog a few basic obedience commands. Some classes even offer the opportunity for your pup to get acquainted with other animals such as cats or horses.

Ask your veterinarian about classes, and look for class postings at the groomer and pet store. It is then a good idea to visit before enrolling your puppy so that you can get an idea about the class atmosphere and personality of the teacher, as well as to find out about age restrictions and inoculation requirements.

> **caution** The puppy will take his signal from your tone of voice and body language. Be calm and speak softly and positively to your pet during veterinary visits. The same goes for your veterinarian. If he or she is rough and gruff and you can't imagine her in the role of your pup's new friend, you might consider a new veterinarian. If you have a needle phobia, recruit another family member to take the puppy to the vet for his vaccinations. Postpone any elective procedures such as neutering or tattooing until the pup is older and past the time when fear has such a lasting effect.

> **note** A second less-defined fear imprint period occurs during a pup's adolescence—ages six to fourteen months. You might notice your dog's reluctance to approach something new or his sudden fear of familiar objects and places. Continue to provide leadership cues and, for now, refrain from forcing him to go beyond his comfort zone

CHAPTER 1 What You Should Know About Your Dog   19

FIGURE 1.3
Your pup's veterinarian is his new best friend.

ARE DOGS EVER TOO YOUNG TO SOCIALIZE?

In the past, veterinarians have been reluctant to recommend that you allow your pup access to other dogs or environments in which dogs congregate until after the puppy has completed his vaccinations against communicable diseases such as distemper and parvovirus. In some instances, vaccinations are not complete until a puppy is four to five months old. If the pup is shielded from novel environments and other dogs during this time, he is missing the prime period for his socialization to both new experiences and to other dogs and people.

Many veterinary behaviorists, including Dr. R.K. Anderson, Professor Emeritus at the College of Veterinary Medicine, University of Minnesota, propose that socialization benefits outweigh the negative potential of disease exposure if the socializing events, puppy classes, for example, take place in an environment in which the risk of disease transmission is low. Check with your veterinarian periodically during the vaccination period to determine if the area where you live and attend puppy classes is free of canine disease outbreaks.

Socializing Your Adolescent Dog

Even if your dog was socialized to people and situations in his puppyhood, he might need a refresher course as he enters adolescence at 6 months of age and continuing through young adulthood, which ends at 18 months. During this period, dogs begin to mature and exert their independence. This might surface as aggression and a testing of your leadership.

Reinforce your dog's socialization to people, other animals, and varied environments. Enrolling him one day a week in doggie day care and/or resuming some of his early obedience training will help him to remember his social skills.

caution Starting at 12 weeks, pups begin testing each other to confirm dominance within their social hierarchy. In other words, they are competing for the pack leader position. This is the Leadership Classification Period. You, of course, are the pack leader of your household, and must make every effort to thwart and stop any type of aggressive behavior, even in play, toward you or others in your household. We'll discuss this topic in greater depth in Chapter 4.

The Flight Instinct Period is the age when your pup will decide it's time to break the apron strings. He is likely to ignore your commands to "come" and just take off for parts unknown. Until you are confident that your dog is trained to obey your commands, you must be extra vigilant to keep him confined to a yard or leash. This misbehavior can become ingrained and harder to correct later if you allow him to escape even once. This period usually lasts two to four weeks and occurs when your pup is four to eight months of age.

Socializing an Older Dog

Dogs who received little exposure to certain types of people, places, or situations as puppies often grow up to exhibit fear when confronted with what to them is an unknown. This was the situation with Gretchen, the Schnauzer you learned about in this book's introduction, who had bonded and lived with Melissa, a single woman. Gretchen was comfortable around other women, but exhibited fear and aggression when forced to associate closely with Melissa's new husband. Men were a different human species as far as this dog was concerned; they were big and loud, and they smelled different from women.

The socialization of older dogs with fears like Gretchen's becomes a lifelong process, one that must proceed slowly and patiently. The procedure involves introducing fear-inducing individuals (dogs or people), places, or situations in a nonthreatening manner using the methods cited next and desensitization techniques (introduced in Chapter 9, "Eliminating Annoying Habits").

Socializing to Dogs

The first step is to find a friendly, playful dog to introduce as a playmate on a frequent and regular basis. If your dog is extremely fearful, a smaller or younger animal might be a good pick for a playmate. Familiarize the dogs in a neutral place such as a park. For the most part, let the dogs interact on their own. If your dog responds by growling or other aggressive behavior, you might have to step in with a loud "no" or instruct your dog to "come" or "sit." (These commands are covered in Chapter 4.) A 10 minute visit is plenty.

> **note** You should consult a professional if your fearful dog is overly aggressive toward family members and strangers. (See "Selecting a Trainer, Behavioral Consultant, or Veterinary Behaviorist" in Appendix A.)

Next time, bring the visiting dog to your home for a play session. Switch homes. When the dogs become comfortable with each other, proceed to take the friends on walks together, where they will be exposed to other dogs at a distance. Next, introduce a second canine playmate and so on in a step by step fashion.

Socializing to People

Socializing your older dog to other people is a gradual process. While the dog is elsewhere, ask the person to be introduced to sit quietly in a comfortable chair in your home. Allow the dog to approach. If the dog contacts the person, have her offer a treat. Praise the dog if he accepts the goodie. Ignore him if he barks or shies away. When possible, introduce one person at a time to your older dog. Work with family members first and regular visitors next in the security of the dog's own home. After your dog becomes accepting of family members, proceed then to introduce strangers on the street or in the park.

To do list

- ❏ Introduce babies to your dog through sounds, sights, and odors
- ❏ Introduce a dog to family members
- ❏ Introduce a new dog to your resident pet

Making Introductions

Our family profiles change. We might start out as a single person, and then marry and have children, who later leave home. We might divorce and remarry, or our elderly parents might come to live with us. Our pet household changes, too; we might start life with a goldfish and then find ourselves adding a dog, another dog, or a cat. Although throwing all the ingredients together makes for good goulash, throwing people and pets together without prior preparation and planning rarely makes for a congenial mix.

Things You'll Need

- ❑ Your dog
- ❑ Willing friend and his/her baby
- ❑ Baby toys, diapers, and other items (if appropriate)
- ❑ Preparing Fido CD
- ❑ Articles of your family's clothing (if appropriate)
- ❑ Dog treats, toys, and leash

Preparing Your Dog for Baby

If your dog was socialized to babies, toddlers, and children when he was in that critical learning period, your road is going to be easier than if your dog has never been around children. But whether it is a refresher course or a new experience for your dog, introducing a baby should take place long before the infant, crying and demanding instant attention, arrives at your home.

Before the arrival of the baby to your home, prepare your dog through his senses of smell, hearing, and sight. You will be setting up the baby's room, anyway, and this is the time to let the dog become acquainted with the aroma of baby powder, formula, and diapers; the sounds of a baby cooing and crying and the jingles of baby rattles and crib mobiles. Allow your pet to see and smell the new equipment—changing table, crib, diaper bag, and so on.

If you have a friend or other family member with a baby, you might ask him or her to bring the baby to your home for a baby rehearsal. The dog should be elsewhere when you bring the infant into the house. You and the baby can then be settled quietly (well, maybe) into a nice rocking chair when your spouse or other family member enters with the dog, restrained on leash. You resume cuddling and cooing with the infant while your family member strokes and speaks soothingly to your pet. Switch places—you cuddle your pet while your family member interacts with the baby. The goal is to have the dog associate the baby with more, not less, attention from family members. Reward good behavior with praise and treats; ignore misbehavior.

caution No matter how trusted your canine companion, he should *never* be left alone with a baby or small child.

note Animal Behavior Associates, Inc. at 303-932-9092 or www.animalbehaviorassociates.com/training-preparing-fido.htm offers a Compact Disk (CD) with a collection of baby sounds to help socialize your dog to babies. It is appropriately named Preparing Fido and includes a helpful "tips" booklet.

CHAPTER 1   What You Should Know About Your Dog

Reinforce obedience command training with your dog. After you bring your own baby home, the dog is going to be intensively curious about the new arrival. Have treats on hand and in place to reward your pet's good behavior around the infant. I know how hard it is to find a spare moment with a new baby at home, but make an effort to spend a few minutes each day with your dog, talking to and reassuring him of his importance to the family. When visitors arrive to dote on the baby, provide them with a new pet toy or treat; if visitors give your dog these treats, your pet won't feel completely left out or banished to the backyard every time the baby is made the center of attention.

> **caution** The baby's safety should be your primary concern. Ensure that your pet is healthy by taking him to the veterinarian for a physical examination, parasite check, and vaccinations before the baby arrives. Most important, never leave a baby and dog together unsupervised.

Introducing a New Dog to Your Children and Other Family Members

Choose a small area of your home, yard, or patio for the planned introduction. Select an article of clothing belonging to each family member (not one that has been freshly laundered) and scatter it around the meeting place. Allow the dog to become familiar with this confined area and the individual smell of each family member. Next, arrange the first face-to-face encounter. (This can be later the same day or the next day.)

Restrain the dog on a leash, and have one adult member of the family loosely control the leash. Invite the child or children to join you on the patio or selected room; instruct them to remain calm and quiet while interacting with the dog. Kneel or sit by the youngsters, and offer your outstretched hand, palm up, toward the dog. Let the dog approach you and sniff your hand. If the dog is willing, scratch him gently on the chest. Let the children mimic your actions. If the meeting goes well, plan a longer visit for later in the day. In the meantime, forbid the children from visiting the dog unattended.

Introducing a New Puppy or Dog to Your Current Pet

When introducing a new dog to your resident dog, arrange the first meeting at a neutral place not associated by either pet as personal territory. This can be a park, a friend's yard, or doggy day care. Have both pets on a loose leash. Make this initial introduction brief (5–10 minutes). Allow the dogs to greet each other.

Dog greets dog with inquisitive sniffing of noses and muzzles. This is the equivalent of our greeting, "Hi, Mary." If they establish that the contact is friendly, they proceed to inspect their individual inguinal (groin) areas, and finally go on to sniff anuses. This three-step greeting process is illustrated in Figure 1.4; I suppose that we can compare it to our shaking hands or patting shoulders.

FIGURE 1.4
Greeting behavior in dogs is ritualized, driven for the most part by each dog's exquisite sense of smell.

If you have the option, arrange short meetings over a period of several days. After you bring the new dog home, confine him in a room or crate where he is visually isolated from other pets. Occasionally, confine resident pets and allow the new dog access to the house so that he can become accustomed to its smells, sounds, and sights.

Make sure that dogs are on leash when they are allowed to greet each other within your home. Within a couple of days, feed the dogs together in the same room, at the same time, but with separate bowls. If one dog refuses to let the other eat, you might have to separate them at feeding time for awhile. Do this quietly without loudly reprimanding the dominant dog; you want him to associate the presence of the new dog or puppy with good things, not constant punishment or verbal admonishments. It usually takes about two weeks for dogs to establish social order at home.

INTRODUCING A CAT INTO A DOG HOUSEHOLD

Dogs and cats have a natural animosity—right? Not necessarily. It depends on the socialization of both species. The ideal match is one in which puppies and kittens are raised together when they are both at that impressionable age (2–7 weeks for kittens; 3–12 weeks for puppies). For pets of any age, follow these steps to introduce your resident dog to his new kitty housemate:

* With animals confined in separate rooms, expose both animals to items with the other animal's scent (toys, blankets, and so on).

* Switch places—allow the cat to roam the dog's spaces while the dog inspects the room containing the cat's carrier, blanket, and litter box.

* Take your dog for a walk to work off excess energy prior to his first face to face with the cat. Set up introductions in a room offering several escape routes for the cat. Restrain the dog on a leash and, if there is doubt about his prey drive, muzzle him. Place your dog in a sitting or down position and allow the cat to approach the dog at his own pace. Be sure that your cat's claws are trimmed. Address each pet by name and talk reassuringly to both. If either animal behaves aggressively, move them to separate rooms until they are calm, and then try again later.

* When the cat and dog exhibit acceptable behavior, release the dog to walk around with his leash still attached so that you can control him. Don't leave them alone together until you are convinced that they can tolerate each other. Make the cat's litter box off-limits to the dog with a baby gate. Provide separate food and water bowls, sleeping areas, and high perches for the cat.

Some dogs with a high prey drive are absolutely resistant to living with cats. Perhaps the worst combination is a dog with a high prey drive (Pit Bull, Rottweiler, Husky, or Malamute breeding, for example) who has never been socialized to cats. Corrections for prey aggression are discussed in Chapter 10, "Getting Tough About Serious Offenses." You also might want to consult a professional trainer or veterinary behaviorist (see Appendix A for professional resources).

Summary

By now, you should have an idea of the factors influencing your dog's or dogs' personalities and perhaps a greater understanding of the type of canine companion that will be a best fit for your home situation. If you and your dog seem mismatched, don't despair. You might not be able to change his physical characteristics, but you can shape his personality through socialization discussed in this chapter and by proper training that we'll explore in Part II, "Train Your Dog or Puppy in No Time," of this book.

If you are contemplating puppy adoption or own a new puppy, you have the keys for socializing him to become the friendly, self-assured dog that you always wanted for your family dog. You can be confident that introducing a new pet or family member to your existing pet family can proceed with minimal disruption by taking a few precautions and safety or guiding steps. Let's now proceed to explore what you should know about dog training.

What You Should Know About Training

In this chapter:

* Determining the best training methods for your dog
* Laying the foundations—selecting who, when, and where for training
* Learning basic training principals

Chapter 1, "What You Should Know About Your Dog," focuses on your dog's background, and how his age, gender, breed ancestry, and socialization opportunities influence his behavior. In this chapter, we ascertain your dog's aptitude for learning certain tasks and discover how training and learning impact his conduct.

Your dog learns primarily from you, other family members, and his home environment. He takes his cues from you—not necessarily what you say but what you imply through tone of voice and body language. It is very important that the signals you send are those you intend and that the home you provide your dog is conducive to learning good manners.

We'll establish the foundations for your training exercises by deciding who should be the primary trainer and choosing the locations and time for training. We'll also explore the basic tenets of training your dog—how to praise him, how to motivate him to acceptable behavior, how to correct misbehavior, and how to gear your training methods to fit his personality.

Train Your Dog In No Time

To do list

- ❑ Understand how breeding affects your dog's learning of specific tasks
- ❑ Determine where your dog falls in the dominance hierarchy

Determining Your Dog's Aptitudes and Training Needs

Dogs differ in their ability to pick up training lessons easily and quickly. They are individuals, requiring different types of human leadership and training tactics.

Your Dog's Aptitude for Learning

All dogs can be trained, but some require more effort than others. Differences in breed aptitudes for learning certain tasks are related to the function for which the dog was originally bred. Shepherds were developed to herd and guard; they readily take up tasks such as heeling and guard dog duties. Retrievers easily learn to "fetch." Conversely, a hound who excels at hunting will take a little longer than his shepherd or retriever friends to learn heeling and fetching. Terriers were originally bred to ferret out rodents and badgers. They are excellent at high-energy tasks such as chasing Frisbees, but usually require extra diligence when toilet training them. These are generalizations, of course, but might give you a clue as to why your dog takes to certain training tasks easily while showing resistance to others.

Breeding is only one factor influencing the ease at which your dog picks up specific tasks. Like us, dogs are individuals and learn at different rates. Perseverance and patience on your part make up the difference if your dog is less skilled at training lessons than the Lassie of old movie reruns.

Using Body Language to Discern Your Dog's Training Needs

Where your dog falls in the leadership hierarchy influences the methods that work best for training. Is your dog shy or submissive? A take-charge, dominant individual? Playful extrovert? A sociable, wanting-to-please type? Temperament tests discussed in Chapter 1 offer one clue. Another is your dog's body language.

As shown in Figure 2.1, dogs demonstrate their personality through their body language. A fearful or submissive dog will try to look

note An extensive explanation of canine body language, including illustrations, is found at www.petfinder.org/journal/docs/CanineBody.pdf.

CHAPTER 2 **What You Should Know About Training** 29

smaller when faced with a perceived threat. He might lie on his back, exposing his genitals; he averts his eyes. A dominant dog will become as large as possible; he stares at you or another dog. The dog competing for pack leader will stand over another dog; he might shove you out of the way to get to the door first. Other dogs fall somewhere in between the two extremes of dominance and submissiveness, and I've categorized their personalities as sociable, easygoing and playful, outgoing.

FIGURE 2.1
Your dog will tell you by his body language where he falls in the canine pecking order.

Living closely with a canine companion gives you insight into your dog's nature. Use Table 2.1 to determine his training needs and the kind of leadership you or someone else in your household should provide to shape him into the perfect dog.

To do list

- ❑ Review the three types of training and choose those you will incorporate into your dog's training program
- ❑ Select a family member to be your dog's primary trainer
- ❑ Enlist family support for training
- ❑ Start checking out places within your home or yard to conduct training exercises
- ❑ Set aside a segment of time for training your dog

Table 2.1 Matching Dog with Trainer and Techniques

Canine Temperament	Training Needs	Training Leader
Submissive, timid, shy, or fearful.	Structured, quiet environment. Reassurance and companionship. Soft voice and gentle touch. Avoid punishment.	Sensitive adult. Limit exposure to loud, rough adults or boisterous children.
Sociable, easygoing.	Consistent and clear leadership.	Your entire family can play a part in training this dog.
Playful, outgoing, curious.	Needs exercise and regular training to keep attention focused on correct behavior.	Responds to active, confident owners. Might prove too energetic for small children or sedentary seniors.
Dominant, self-assured. Can be provoked to bite, growl, or fight.	Firm, forthright leadership. Immediate and decisive correction.	Responds to knowledgeable, self-assured adults. Not for indecisive individuals, children, or sedentary seniors.
Dominant, aggressive. Easily provoked to bite, growl, or attack.	Professional training.	Responds to structured programs such as those provided for guard or police dogs.

Integrating Training Methods into Family Life

Although the lines blur, training can be divided into manners training, obedience training, and activity training. *Manners* training teaches your dog good behavior around others and your property. A dog who begs at the table, rushes the door ahead of you, and chews your loafers is definitely not acting mannerly toward you or your "stuff."

Obedience training involves teaching your dog to perform specific tasks in response to basic commands such as "sit" or "come" when you give a verbal or hand signal. *Activity* training is the means by which you teach your dog to perform certain jobs or leisure activities such as catching a Frisbee or "playing dead."

Teaching all forms of training ensures your dog's safety and makes his life (and yours) more pleasurable. A dog focused on catching a fly ball is not going to be barking excessively at the back gate or digging in the garden. Teaching your dog to "come" and "sit" when he noses around a prickly cactus or prepares to chase a squirrel across the street stops an accident in progress.

I encourage you to select activities that you and your family enjoy and incorporate them into your dog's manners and obedience training program.

CHAPTER 2   What You Should Know About Training

Things You'll Need

- ❏ Your dog
- ❏ Meeting place for family conferences
- ❏ Chalk or cork board for posting training rules
- ❏ Pencil, paper, chalk, or push pins

Selecting a Head Trainer

Select one person from your household to be your dog's primary trainer. This person will be the pack leader from the dog's point of view. Some dogs balk at accepting children as pack leader. If your teenager is the dog owner, give consideration to his personality and level of maturity, as well as dominance traits of the dog, before assigning him to the head trainer position. Review Table 2.1 to determine which family member best suits the requirements for training your dog. In most cases, this will be you or your spouse.

Family cooperation is essential so that you will all be singing the same tune when it comes to training. If you forbid your dog from lying on the couch, all family members should refrain from allowing the dog access to the couch. As demonstrated in Figure 2.2, discussing each of your training rules at regular family meetings will ensure training harmony. Each time you introduce a new "word" or command, you must tell the family about it and post a notice that everyone can examine at leisure. After your pet learns a particular lesson, other family members should reinforce correct behavior.

Where to Train

Begin training within your home or in the backyard, preferably in a location that is relatively free of distractions. One of your first instructions is teaching your puppy to go potty in a certain area in response to a command such as "potty." (Choosing your dog's toilet training spaces will be covered in Chapter 3, "Getting Ready for Training.") After your puppy becomes proficient with at-home toilet training, encourage him to "potty" in the correct location at highway rest stops or dog parks. In that way, you are reinforcing lessons in different locations with varying levels of activity going on around you.

Although toilet training is associated with a particular location, other commands can be cued at almost any place. You can teach your dog to

note *Training Tip* — Show your dog that you are pack leader by going through doors and passageways first. Eat your meals before feeding your dog, and ban begging at the dining table. If your dog is blocking your path, instruct him to move out of your way; don't step around or over him. Establishing your alpha position teaches your dog to respect your authority.

"sit" in the kitchen, in the backyard, and at the schoolyard. Once the dog understands the "words" and accompanying action, he should be able to perform them, regardless of locality, in response to your instruction.

FIGURE 2.2
Family meetings ensure consistency with training methods and rules.

When to Train

Set aside a regular time for training. This will be a short period (5–15 minutes) when your attention is focused on your relationship with your dog and the lessons you are teaching him. Put aside the cell phone and let the recorder answer the house telephone. Your dog deserves your full concentration during your scheduled time together.

In addition to the scheduled training period, incorporate training into your daily life. You might place your dog's bed and a couple of toys in front of the television. During commercial breaks, you can instruct the dog to respond to one of your command sequences such as "sit," followed by "stay." Ask your pet to "sit" before you feed him or to "sit" before

> **note** The time you spend on formal training should be geared to your dog's attention span. Puppies require shorter periods than adults. Multiple 5- to 10-minute training sessions per day are more productive than one 20- or 30-minute session.

CHAPTER 2 What You Should Know About Training   33

you throw the Frisbee. Integrate training into daily life with your pet in such a way that training, exercising, and playing are indistinguishable.

To do list

- ❏ Learn to communicate clearly with your dog
- ❏ Become skilled at giving immediate feedback to your dog's actions
- ❏ Discover ways that you or other family members might be undermining your dog's training success
- ❏ Decide the one name you will ask your dog to respond to

Learning the Rules of Training

Following the rules of training saves time by guaranteeing that everyone involved with training your dog is operating on the same wavelength. By being true to these rules, you are showing respect for your dog and ensuring that he succeeds in learning training lessons.

Sending a Clear Message

Training will go much easier if all family members send a clear, consistent message when interacting with your dog.

Your dog learns from you by observing your body language, facial expressions, and voice tone. In general, a command should sound serious, not frivolous. Keep your actions and feelings in sync and appropriate to the task at hand. Don't correct while smiling or giggling. When you say "no" to your dog, your voice should be pitched deeper than when you use "good." Your dog learns from your voice that you are pleased or displeased.

Consistency with the use of language, commands, and training methods avoids uncertainty. "Sit" and "down" are two commands. Using "sit down" as a command presents your dog with a puzzle. Is he supposed to sit on his haunches or flop down? If you use "down" to tell your dog to assume a position, do not use this word to correct jumping up behavior. (I will introduce the first words that you will use to communicate with your dog in Chapter 4, "Manners Training: Week by Week.")

If you call your dog with "Rover, come," use it each and every time you or someone else calls

tip It is easier for your dog to learn his name if you choose a short one- or two-syllable name such as Rover, rather than using his registered name of Red Rover of Palm Beach Kennel. Avoid nicknames such as Snookums or Damn Dog, if these are not his name. Too many names are as confusing as too long a name.

him. Yelling "Come on over, Red Rover," might amuse the neighborhood kids but is also likely to confuse your dog.

Giving Immediate Feedback

Reinforcing your dog's proper behavior with praise or reward, and correcting misbehavior with negative reinforcement or punishment, teaches him how to win your approval and how to avoid your disapproval. Responding immediately gives him instant feedback and enables him to make the association between his actions and your reaction.

Offering Positive Reinforcement

Positive reinforcement ensures that your dog's accomplishments are noted and encouraged, thus increasing the likelihood that they will occur again. The reinforcer is an object or action that the dog wants, such as a toy, treat, petting, or praise.

If you notice your dog doing something right—playing gently with his new kitty friend or waiting until you enter the doorway first—give him immediate feedback. He knows from your tone of voice, the smile on your face, and the verbal response "good" that you are pleased. Go one step further by actively searching for appropriate behavior to reward.

Correct timing is essential for the success of reinforcement training. Whatever you are offering as the inducement should occur in conjunction with or within seconds of the correct behavior. Reinforcing too early or too late encourages whatever is occurring at the time you offer the reward. If you are teaching your puppy to sit, for example, give the command "Rover, sit." When the puppy sits, you offer praise, petting, or a small bite of cheese (or all three). If you get distracted and the pup is standing before you offer praise or treat, he thinks that you are rewarding him for standing. If you say "good" while he is sitting, and offer the cheese while he is standing, you've violated the "Send a Clear Message" rule.

Correcting Misbehavior

Negative reinforcement is something a dog will work to avoid. You pull on the dog's leash (negative reinforcement) and stop when he comes along. Punishment as a correction is a negative consequence for a certain action. Showing your disapproval with a frown and with a loud admonishing "no" will be punishment enough for most dogs.

For punishment to be effective, it must coincide with or take place within one or two seconds of the misbehavior. Squirting the puppy with a water pistol when you catch him gnawing your new slippers is effective as a training technique only if you catch him in the destructive act. Chapter 4 offers more appropriate ideas for dealing with puppy chewing.

CHAPTER 2 What You Should Know About Training

Making Training Fair and Fun

You want your dog to be successful in learning correct behavior. Don't set him up for failure by leaving the thawing steak on the counter in front of his food bowl or the package of doggy treats you use for training rewards on the coffee table. Have the children put Raggedy Ann back in the closed toy box rather than leaving it where your puppy might be tempted to mouth Ann's stringy red hair.

It is unfair to expect your dog to do something that frightens him or is beyond his capabilities. If he has an aversion to loud noises, don't ask him to accompany you to the park to watch the Fourth of July fireworks until he has received treatment for his noise phobia. If your dog is old and toothless, refrain from teaching him to "fetch" the cold beer can.

> **note** Exercise patience with your dog and yourself. Few of us—human or canine—learn new tasks in one session. Your dog will need repeated instruction and constant supervision, especially when he is first learning a new behavior. If you are having a rough day and find yourself becoming over harried or disgruntled, postpone training for later in the day. Balance adhering to a schedule with being a positive influence on your dog.

Training Tip

End training on an upbeat note by instructing your dog to perform a task that you know he has mastered. In that way, you finish the session with a reward of praise or treat. Follow a training session by taking your pet on a walk or by playing a game with him. He will be rewarded for success and have fun with you, his pack leader.

Summary

Your dog is an expert at nonverbal language. He lets you know what he is feeling by displaying certain predictable body postures. Save training time by learning to read your dog's behavior. In the same way, your dog comprehends your feelings by closely observing your emotions as recorded in your tone of voice and body language cues. Ensure that your verbal and nonverbal messages agree. With improved communication, training proceeds as quickly as your dog's intelligence and temperament allow.

Provide your dog with leadership. He is reassured by knowing that you are the alpha pack member and that he can look to you for guidance. He wants to please you. Capitalize on his need for your approval by giving instant and appropriate feedback to his actions.

Incorporate training into daily life by enlisting all household members to work as a unit and by reinforcing training tasks during small tidbits of time spent watching TV or going for a walk. Attention to training rules ensures that your dog reaches his full potential as a valued family member.

Getting Ready for Training

I'm old enough to remember when displays of canine training gear at veterinary clinics and pet stores offered a limited selection of collars, leashes, and a few chew toys. Our choices today for pet training equipment seem endless, and it's easy to become overwhelmed and confused when you visit a pet super store or even peruse the pet section of eBay.

You don't need to own the latest in gadgetry to train your dog. It's more important that you form the proper leadership role with your dog than that you attempt to coerce him with a shock collar or ultrasonic device.

In this chapter, you learn about some of the equipment and supplies you'll want to have on hand when you begin training your dog. I'm going to be conservative and suggest basic equipment, and, where appropriate, alert you to products that you might consider if your budget allows for extras in the dog care arena or if your friends are hosting a shower for your new pooch.

In this chapter:

* Preparing your dog's living spaces
* Buying the equipment and supplies you will need for training

To do list

- ❏ Choose a crate or dog house
- ❏ Select a potty training method
- ❏ Decide on an area in your home and/or yard in which to locate your dog's toilet

Preparing Your Dog's Spaces

A wild or domesticated canine establishes a den—a place to feel safe, snug, and protected from the outside world. For the most part, your pet's den will be a crate, kennel, or dog house. His territory, which is the space he will guard from intruders, may extend to the entire house or backyard. His bathroom will be located in an area you select within this territory.

Things You'll Need

- ❏ Crate, kennel, bed, or dog house
- ❏ Exercise pen or baby gate
- ❏ Water and food bowls
- ❏ Chew toys
- ❏ Treats
- ❏ Soft towel or fleece baby blanket

Choosing and Locating the Crate

A crate (plastic, wire, or soft sided) becomes your puppy's den within your home. We want to take advantage of a dog's natural tendency to keep his den clean. Wild dogs and wolves eliminate in a place outside their den and away from where they eat and sleep.

Purchase a crate commensurate with the size of your dog or puppy. It should be large enough for the dog to stand up, turn around, and lie down comfortably, but refrain from buying the Taj Mahal model. You don't want the dog to think he has enough space to eliminate in one end of his crate and eat and sleep in the other. If you own a large breed puppy, you might have to buy a series of crates over time to allow for his increasing size, or, opt for a crate with dividers.

CHAPTER 3 Getting Ready for Training

I suggest that you put the crate in an area of your home which is close to family activity without being in the middle of the action. You might find a space within the laundry room, kitchen, or mud room that will accommodate the crate. Most of these rooms have the added advantage of smooth, easily cleaned flooring. Enclose the room with a baby gate or use expandable exercise pens to create a puppy playpen within the room.

As seen in Figure 3.1, make the pup's crate welcoming by adding a soft towel or blanket. Later, you will introduce your dog to his new den by placing his water/feed bowls, toys, and treats inside.

> **caution** Never bring a new dog into your home and allow him free access to the house. Confine him to a crate or to one room of the house. Expand his territory gradually and only when you are available to monitor his manners. Prepare your home by removing objects that might be toxic to or be swallowed by your pet.

FIGURE 3.1
Your puppy's crate is his home within your home.

Choosing and Locating the Dog House

Many of the same principles for selecting/placing a crate apply to selecting and placing a dog house. You can opt for a generic plastic igloo, or you can design or purchase a dog house resembling your own home or Cinderella's castle. Regardless, the house you select ought to be an appropriate size for your dog and protect him from the outside elements.

The dog should be able to stand up and look out the door without crouching and should be able to stretch out in a comfortable sleeping position. Locate the house in a well-drained area of the yard or patio and avoid facing it toward the prevailing wind or setting sun.

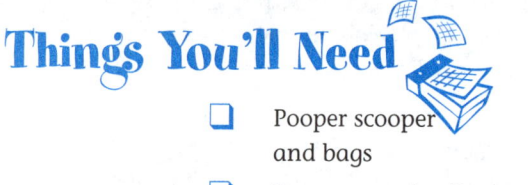

Things You'll Need

- ❑ Pooper scooper and bags
- ❑ Paper or canine litter or sod box system

Preparing for Yard, Paper, or Litter Box Training

One of the first acts of training you and your puppy or dog embark on together is that of toilet training. Choose the method you use carefully. Puppies that are paper and litter box trained can be taught later to go outside in the yard or park; however, surface (substrate) preferences imprinted early in life might be difficult to change at a later date.

Selecting an Outside Toilet

Choose a location in your yard that will be used specifically as the dog's potty, and give preference to an area that is a direct route out one of your home's doors. You will want to use the same door every time you take your puppy outside as you want him to learn to associate the act of going out the door and walking to this particular spot with the act of "going potty."

Paper and Litter or Sod Boxes

If you live in a high-rise apartment, have adopted a puppy during inclement weather, or want to avoid taking your dog outside late at night, consider training him to eliminate on paper or in a litter box or sod container.

> **caution** If you select paper training, don't line the dog's crate or bed with paper products.

CHAPTER 3   Getting Ready for Training   41

YARD CONCERNS FOR DOG OWNERS

Dog urine and feces might have a fertilizer effect on grass called "greening up" or might cause the grass to burn, creating dead, brown patches. Urine is a bigger culprit than feces because urine is absorbed into the ground quicker.

To offset these potential problems, remove fecal deposits as soon as possible and water your yard after the dog has eliminated to dilute the urine effect.

A creative solution is to design an area specifically for dog waste. Remove the grass in this area and replace with a substrate that your dog likes such as artificial turf, pea-gravel, or mulch. Be creative and add a faux fireplug or large boulder to act as a marking post for male dogs.

If you choose newspapers or commercial potty training pads for your paper system, place them inside a small contained area opposite your puppy's crate and feeding and water bowls. Keep the papers in the same location, and place a damp bottom paper on top of the new ones when you change papers to provide an odor clue that this is indeed the bathroom.

Second nature by Purina is an inexpensive litter box system for small dogs (less than $20 for pan and instructions at most pet stores). The litter is larger than that used for cats and is made from absorbent paper. Boxes come in three sizes with the largest accommodating dogs up to thirty-five pounds. Place the box near the dog's crate or bed but not directly adjacent to it. Define your dog's territory, containing his crate/bed and litter pan, using your expandable exercise panels or baby gate.

A California company named PetaPotty offers a canine sod-based system, as shown in Figure 3.2. This company makes several container sizes that can be placed adjacent to each other to form a toilet system for larger dogs. You select real or artificial grass turf for the substrate material.

When your dog urinates in the box, waste drains through the turf and into a concealed trap pan. It is recommended that you flush the sod with water from a hose or bucket several times per week. Solid waste should be scooped and flushed down your commode. Depending on the size of dog and number of dogs using the system, you will have to replace grass sod every couple of months. The PetaPotty can be placed on a boat deck, patio or balcony, or within the apartment itself.

tip If you will be training your dog to go outside at a later date, prepare the dog for that surface. You might lay down a couple of concrete tiles under the papers or litter if you will eventually instruct an urban dog to eliminate curbside. If you intend the dog to eliminate on grass, rub grass and a little dirt into the training pad or papers.

42 Train Your Dog In No Time

FIGURE 3.2
Consider PetaPotty's sod container system for dogs confined on boats or in high-rise apartments.

Fetch

For more information about PetaPotty, call (866) 738-7297 or visit the company's website at www.petapotty.com. This system ranges in cost from $180 to $260.

To do list

- ☐ Choose collars and leash
- ☐ Buy treats and toys
- ☐ Select cleaning supplies

Buying Equipment and Supplies

Preparing for a new dog is similar to planning a baby's layette. You need to accumulate certain supplies before bringing the new puppy or dog home.

CHAPTER 3 **Getting Ready for Training**   43

Things You'll Need

- [ ] Collars, leash, and ID tag
- [ ] Treats, Kongs, and other toys
- [ ] Cleaning supplies for potty accidents

Choosing a Collar and Leash

You will need a basic cotton web, nylon, or leather rolled or flat collar with a buckle or snap-together clasp of the appropriate size for your dog. Collars come in half-inch lengths. If your dog has a lot of hair, the collar should fit under the coat and close to the skin. You should be able to slip one finger between the dog's skin and collar for small dogs and about two fingers under the collar of larger dogs.

A nylon slip collar, which tightens around the dog's neck, is effective for certain training exercises in which you really need to get your dog's attention. Measure the neck and add three inches for proper length. The collar should be just long enough to fit over the dog's head. To use this type of collar, give it a fast tighten and then just a quick release. If pressure on the neck is contraindicated (dogs with medical conditions affecting the neck), make do with the buckle collar or opt for a head collar or no-pull training harness.

> **note** Some trainers are opposed to slip collars, especially the chain variety, because they can be used to "choke" the dog. Head collars and no-pull harnesses avoid the neck area by tightening around the dog's head in the former and his chest and shoulder blades in the latter case. See Chapter 5, "Graduating to Next-Level Basics," for a discussion of these training aids.

For most situations, a four- or six-foot leather or cotton web leash is sufficient. The snap bolt should be the proper size for your dog. A toy dog dragging around a long leash with a heavy bolt is handicapped; conversely, you will be handicapped if you try to train a huge dog with a flimsy leash with a tiny snap bolt.

Even if your dog has permanent identity data such as a microchip or tattoo, attach an ID tag with your name, telephone number, and address to his collar when he travels outside your home.

Figure 3.3 shows some examples of these basic training supplies.

Selecting Treats

In Chapter 2, "What You Should Know About Training," we discussed using treats and praise or petting as positive reinforcement for encouraging your dog to perform an action. When you use food to persuade a beginner, reinforce the desired behavior each time it occurs. If you are training your puppy to sit on command, you must offer him a treat, such as a tidbit of weenie, and praise/petting each time he performs correctly.

After he has mastered the trick, the food reward can be used intermittently and eventually phased out so that the puppy will perform for praise and petting alone.

FIGURE 3.3
You'll need buckle (1) and training (2) collars, plus leash (3), and ID (4) tag.

Training Tip
When using food as a positive reinforcer, present the smallest amount that will encourage your dog to perform. If the pup is particularly fond of liver snaps, give him a morsel (not the entire cookie) for correct execution of a simple task. This allows for more reinforcements per training session before the dog becomes full. Animal trainer Karen Pryor says that the reward should be based on the difficulty of the task. If your puppy makes a major training breakthrough—he comes when called off leash for the first time—reward him with the jackpot of a whole cookie.

TREATS

Here are some examples of treats you might use while training your dog:

Piece of dry cat food or puppy kibble	Bite of regular ration
Small cube of cheese	Commercial treat
Morsel of weenie/Vienna sausage	Cooked meatball
Tidbit of hard-boiled egg	Piece cooked, boneless chicken or fish

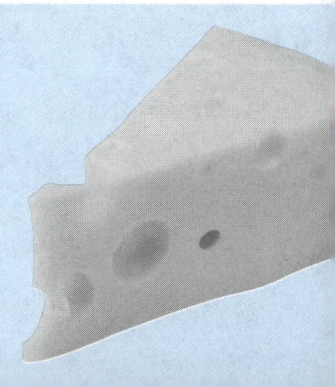

CHAPTER 3   Getting Ready for Training

What You Should Know About Toys

Toys should be appropriate to your dog's size, activity level, and chewing preferences. In general, provide your dog with a variety of toys and rotate them weekly by offering only a few of the playthings at a time. Observe toys carefully, removing and destroying any that have become unsafe (due to cracking, unraveling, losing stuffing, and so on).

Items you might consider for your dog's toy box include

- Interactive toys such as balls or Frisbees.
- Objects for safe chewing and carrying around. These include hard, rubber toys such as Nylabone "bones" and Kong products available in a variety of shapes and sizes.
- Distraction toys include the Kongs and "busy boxes" with hiding places for treats; your dog gets to the goodies by moving or nosing the toy with his paws or muzzle (see Figure 3.4).
- Rope toys are available in various shapes with knotted ends and can provide a flossing action for teeth.
- Comfort toys (stuffed toys, for example) might be appropriate for certain dogs.

caution Select treats that are harmless to your pet. Avoid salty foods for dogs suffering from heart problems and select low-calorie treats for overweight dogs.

caution All dog toys can be abused. Toys too small, too flimsy, or fitted with squeakers, strings, eyes, or other attached items might be swallowed, leading to intestinal obstruction. Certain dogs can even misuse hard toys by chewing to the point of cracking teeth or by ingesting big chunks of rawhide or other material, leading to constipation or impaction.

FIGURE 3.4
Toys stuffed with food treats are great boredom relievers for your pet.

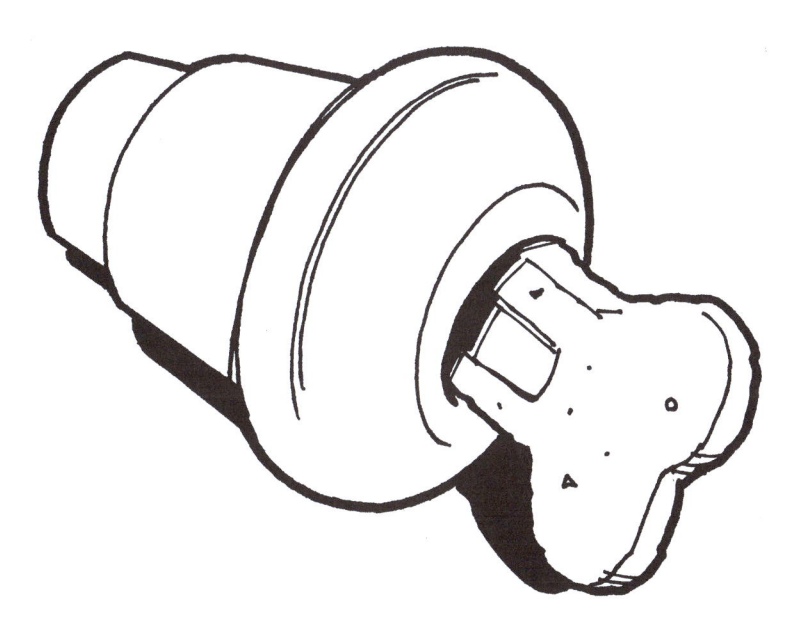

Selecting Cleaning Products for Training Accidents

Dogs can detect elimination odors imperceptible to us and, in many cases, are compelled to reapply urine or feces to the soiled area. In some cases, pet residues have been left by previously-owned pets, and in others the dog is reinforcing his own scent.

Regardless, it is important to neutralize and remove any trace odor of urine and feces so that the puppy or dog is not attracted back to urinate and defecate. After blotting with paper towels, apply a cleaning product containing natural enzymes to completely remove urine or fecal deposits.

Numerous enzymatic cleaners are available for purchase online or at stores. Urine-Off products are available at www.urine-off.com and Anti-Icky-Poo at www.mistermax.com or by calling (800) 745-1671.

note In many cases, the lines blur between toys and treats. Kong and Nylabone companies offer products that provide both features. Visit Kong at www.kongcompany.com or (303) 216-2626 and Nylabone at www.nylabone.com or (800) 631-2188.

caution Avoid cleaning products containing ammonia because they leave an odor similar to that of urine.

Summary

In this chapter, you've gotten ready for training by purchasing or acquiring the equipment you'll need. You've prepared the home and yard so that toilet and house training proceeds quickly and efficiently.

You've equipped your dog with collars and leash, selected treats and toys for relieving boredom and for rewarding proper behavior, and anticipated accidents by adding enzymatic solutions to your repertoire of cleaning supplies. In the next chapter, we start the actual training process. I hope that you are ready and raring to go.

Part II

Train Your Dog or Puppy In No Time

4   Manners Training: Week by Week **49**

5   Graduating to Next-Level Basics **71**

6   Having Fun with Simple Tricks **85**

7   Having Fun While Exercising **93**

4

Manners Training: Week by Week

In this chapter:

* Learning to choose and use verbal commands
* Introducing the crate
* House training your dog
* Presenting basic obedience commands (sit and come) and curbing unwanted biting and chewing
* Beginning leash training
* Teaching down, stay, and a release word

In this chapter, we get right to the nuts and bolts of manners and obedience training. This is where we apply the rules of training presented in Chapter 2, "What You Should Know About Training," and use the equipment and supplies suggested in Chapter 3, "Getting Ready for Training."

I will offer training tasks as a six-week course. If your dog loves his crate and is acceptably house trained, you might want to review "Choosing and Using Commands" in Week One and start your primary training at Week Two.

Regardless of where you begin, remember to set aside a regular time for training and to keep training sessions short (5–15 minutes once or twice a day/6 days a week). In addition, incorporate past and current training tasks into daily interactions with your pet. In this way, you will be reinforcing lessons multiple times during each day as you feed, play with, and exercise your dog.

To do list

- ❑ Choose and learn to use verbal commands
- ❑ Teach feedback words "good" and "no"
- ❑ Introduce dog to crate
- ❑ Begin house training
- ❑ Accustom your dog to his buckle collar and leash

Week One: Using Commands and Beginning Basic Crate and House Training

During Week One, you will begin using commands with your dog as you introduce him to his home within your home (his crate), his collar and leash, and house-training rules and schedule. This is a lot of information for your dog to absorb, so you must proceed with devotion to your task and to your canine charge.

Things You'll Need

- ❑ Your dog
- ❑ Crate
- ❑ Exercise pen or baby gate
- ❑ Water and food bowls
- ❑ Chew toys
- ❑ Treats
- ❑ Soft towel or fleece baby blanket
- ❑ Buckle collar and leash
- ❑ Pooper scooper and bags
- ❑ Papers, canine litter, or sod box (for indoor toilet training)

Choosing and Using Commands

Verbal language is not your dog's natural form of communication. Instead, he discerns from your body language, facial expressions, and voice tone what you are trying to communicate. Your actions, expressions, and speech timbre should be in sync with what you are trying to convey verbally.

The brightest dog is capable of learning only a limited vocabulary of words. Keep verbal communication with your dog simple and consistent so that your dog eventually understands the association of a word or set of words with his proper response.

Where possible, use one-syllable words to form the basis of your dog's vocabulary. In Week One, you begin using a few basic command words, such as "crate" and "potty" and the feedback words "good" and "no." *Feedback* words are your most useful tools of guidance, and can stand alone (without using your dog's name) because they should illicit your dog's full and immediate attention.

> **tip** Be generous with the use of "good" because dogs, like people, are motivated by positive reinforcement. Make sure, however, that the timing of the praise coincides with the desired behavior and that you don't confuse the dog by repeating the phrase after the desired action has ceased.

Although it is tempting to use a variety of praise words such as "That's my dog," "You're such a little trooper," and so forth, your dog will learn what you mean quicker if you consistently use the word "good" to affirm your delight and pleasure with his behavior.

It is essential that your dog knows his name. Prefacing your verbal communication with his name gets your dog's attention and alerts him that you are going to tell him what to do. Use his name first, and then give the command; for example, say "Rover, come" or "Rover, crate" rather than "Come, Rover" or "Crate, Rover."

When your puppy responds positively to your command—for example, going in his crate when you say "Rover, crate"—you should immediately and joyously say, "good" or "good dog." It helps, particularly in the early phases of teaching, to reinforce your message with a treat. If your pup fails to respond to your command, don't make a big deal out of it or keep repeating the command. Withhold praise and treat, and walk away. You can try again later when success is more probable.

If you catch your dog in the act of inappropriate behavior—making a puddle on the floor or showing undue interest in the garbage can, for instance—show your displeasure by saying "no."

Crate Training

Using a baby gate or expandable exercise pens, restrict your dog to a small area of your home that contains his crate. Place the dog in this area, and let him explore the crate on his own for a few minutes. Next, prop open the door of the crate and toss in a treat. When you catch him going inside, immediately give the command for going to the crate ("Rover, crate") and praise him lavishly using the feedback word "good." Choose an easy to understand and remember command, such as "crate" or "kennel up." Use that command consistently.

> **caution** As a safety precaution, always remove your dog's collars and leash when leaving him in the crate.

REWARDS AND CORRECTIONS

A primary reward is something that your dog wants (food treat, petting, toys, and so on). A secondary reward is something the dog learns is a reward—the word good, for instance. When you tie the two types of rewards together, the dog learns that "good" is something he should work to obtain from you. Phase out multiple rewards so that the dog is motivated solely by your approval and feedback of "good."

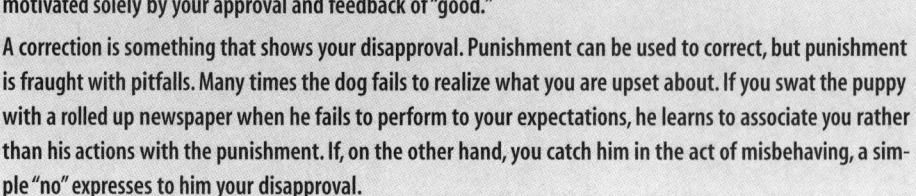

A correction is something that shows your disapproval. Punishment can be used to correct, but punishment is fraught with pitfalls. Many times the dog fails to realize what you are upset about. If you swat the puppy with a rolled up newspaper when he fails to perform to your expectations, he learns to associate you rather than his actions with the punishment. If, on the other hand, you catch him in the act of misbehaving, a simple "no" expresses to him your disapproval.

Rewards and corrections must be appropriate to your dog's actions. If you consistently reward (using treats or words) no matter how he performs, your dog has no incentive to please you. If you correct after the fact, your dog has no way of discerning what he has done wrong.

After your dog has accepted the crate by fearlessly coming and going within its confines, give your crating command and place him inside when it's time for a nap, for feeding, or for bedtime. You can let him out again as soon as he awakens or completes his meal. During the training process, use the crating command and reward your dog with a treat and praise each time he goes into the crate.

If your dog or puppy makes a fuss while in his crate, walk out of the room and ignore him; you don't want to reward barking and scratching by letting him out of the crate. When the dog accepts the crate quietly, you can release him. The exception is when your puppy has been crated for a long period and he is notifying you that he needs to go potty. You will soon learn by his body language (restlessness, circling, scratching at his bedding, whining) that he needs to go.

Your dog's crate is his safe haven from the outside world. For this reason, refrain from using the crate as punishment and instruct the children to leave the puppy alone while he is crated. Confining your puppy to his crate when you are unavailable to supervise will aid you in training him to use an appropriate toilet area.

caution Don't confine your dog or puppy beyond the time he is capable of controlling his bladder and bowels. As a general rule, puppies can be crated the number of hours corresponding to their age in months, plus one. A three-month old can be constrained for a maximum period of four hours. This formula has limits. Nine hours is max for most dogs. Young puppies, elderly dogs, and dogs suffering from certain medical conditions might need to eliminate as often as every one to two hours.

Toilet Training

A puppy normally eliminates when he awakens, after eating and drinking, after play or other activity, and before bedding down in his crate for the evening. Because young puppies' bladders are small, they will also have to go during the night. Usually, the puppy will alert you by whining or crying. You might use a baby monitor in order to respond to your puppy's needs if your bedroom is in a distant location.

Developing a schedule for taking the dog or puppy to eliminate is essential for simplified toilet training. Adhering to this schedule is easier if you offer timed rather than unlimited access to food and water. Provide food for 15 minutes and then take away the feed bowl. (Don't be deterred if the dog has left much of his food.) Wait 5 minutes and offer all the water the dog will drink. Remove the water bowl during the initial stages of toilet training. Later, you will make fresh water available at all times.

If you are away from home for many hours during the day, you might solicit a neighbor or professional pet sitter for help in adhering to a schedule those important first weeks of potty training.

Consider training your puppy to go on paper or in a sod or litter box if you are unavailable during the day for the many trips outside necessary for training small puppies. Remember that puppies develop surface preferences for elimination; you might opt for a sod system if you will later train your dog to eliminate on the grass outside.

SAMPLE SCHEDULE FOR WORKING OWNERS

Adapt the schedule to fit your needs and your dog's needs. A young puppy or geriatric pet might require an additional mid-morning trip to the toilet area. When you are home for holidays and weekends, add socialization and additional training sessions.

6 a.m.: Take dog to toilet area.

6:30 a.m.: Feed, water, and take dog to toilet area, play, exercise.

7 a.m.: Confine dog using crate, baby gate, or exercise pen.

Noon: Feed (puppy), water, and take dog to toilet area, play, exercise. Confine dog before leaving house.

Midafternoon: Water and take dog to toilet area.

Home from work: Water and take dog to toilet area. Obedience training sessions, play, exercise.

Early evening: Feed (puppy or small-breed adult), water, and take dog to toilet area, play, exercise.

Before bedtime: Take dog to toilet area.

Bedtime: Confine dog.

Toilet Training Outside

Attach your dog's collar and leash if you are going outside for toilet training. Lead your dog directly to the toilet area; refuse to let him loiter, sniffing and exploring every bush, along the way. Stand quietly at the designated area while your dog discerns by sight and smell that this is his bathroom.

COLLAR AND LEASH TRAINING IN THREE STEPS

1. Place your pup's buckle collar around his neck while talking soothingly to him. If he shows discomfort, distract him with a toy (Kong filled with peanut butter). Leave the collar on for short periods until the dog wears it without noticing.
2. Attach the clip from a leash to your dog's collar and let him wear it until he adjusts to the extra weight.
3. Add a leash with a clip to your dog's collar and engage your dog with an interactive toy. Encourage the dog to walk around, dragging the leash. Supervise him in case the leash gets caught on something. Continue short training periods until the dog shows no negative reaction to the leash.

When your dog settles down at the designated outdoor toilet area, introduce the potty command, which might be one word such as "potty" or a short phase such as "go potty." You want the dog to associate the command with the actual process of elimination.

When the dog begins to eliminate, use the "good" feedback word. The attention span of a young pup is no longer than thirty seconds, so praise using the "good" word should be given when the dog is actually eliminating. Immediately after your dog finishes, treat and pet him.

Allow a 10-minute period for the dog to relieve himself. If he hasn't done so, return him to his crate or exercise pen and try again in 15 minutes.

When you find evidence of an accident in the crate or confined area, take the pup to another room while you quietly take care of the mess. Don't "rub his nose in it," scold him, or hit him with a newspaper. Clean by blotting or picking up with a paper towel (don't use your foot as you will leave the scent when you walk) and by applying an enzymatic cleaner to completely remove any residue of urine or fecal odor.

If you catch the dog in the process of eliminating in a place other than his toilet area, interrupt with "no" and then immediately take him to the proper place.

CHAPTER 4 Manners Training: Week by Week

Toilet Training Inside

Set up the dog's toilet (papers, pan, or sod containment system) within his confined area. It should be away from but easily accessible to those areas where he sleeps and eats.

If your adult dog has been trained to go outside and you are transitioning him to an indoor system, use sod or wood chips on top of the papers or inside the litter pan. Otherwise, fill the pan about one inch deep with dog litter, as shown in Figure 4.1. Give an odoriferous clue that this is the bathroom by placing a small amount of urine or solid waste on papers or on litter or sod.

FIGURE 4.1
Place your dog in the litter box after crating, eating, exercising, and sleeping.

Adhering to the schedule suggested earlier, take the dog or puppy to the papers, pan, or sod containment box. Give the potty command and offer immediate and lavish praise and a treat for correct behavior. When the dog jumps out of the box without doing his business, pick him up and return him. Give the command once again, and reward him for eliminating. If the dog still doesn't comply within a few minutes, place him back in his crate or confined area and try again later.

To do list

- ❏ Continue crate and toilet training
- ❏ Reinforce your dog's vocabulary
- ❏ Teach your dog to come when called
- ❏ Teach the "sit" command
- ❏ Stop unwanted chewing and biting behavior in puppies

Week Two: Adding Basic Commands and Stopping Unwanted Behaviors

Although it shouldn't take more than a few days to accustom your dog to his crate, teaching accident-proof potty manners is an ongoing process for most owners.

Certain dogs, those bred to retain puppy-like characteristics (Lhasa Apso and Yorkshire Terrier, for example), might take up to three months to catch on to toilet training. Patience and consistency on your part will ensure your dog's eventual success. Continue to use the crating and potty commands. As your dog has fewer accidents and seems more accustomed to the commands and schedule, you can ease off on the use of treats for crating and toilet training and reinforce with the feedback words of "good" and "no."

During this week, we'll add the "come" and "sit" commands and address certain unwanted behaviors. For best results, introduce these commands during your regular scheduled training sessions of 5–15 minutes once or twice a day for six days a week.

note Don't expect 100% success immediately when house training your dog. You might find that you need to periodically retrain your pet or deal with secondary issues such as submissive wetting and occasional accidents. To learn how to successfully tackle these minor road bumps, see Chapter 8, "Housetraining in Every Way."

Things You'll Need

- ❏ Your dog
- ❏ Buckle collar and leash
- ❏ Treats
- ❏ Chew and teething toys
- ❏ Diversion items (pennies in can)
- ❏ Bitter spray

Teaching Your Dog to Come When Called

Teaching your dog to come when called is one of his most important lessons. You can start by enticing him to come for treats. While toilet and crate training, you've probably introduced your dog to liver snaps or other goodies. Take a container with a lid and throw in a few pieces of dry kibble and treats. Allow Rover to join you in the kitchen. Shake the can and say, "Rover, come." When he comes, reward him with a treat. Repeat several times a day for two or three days.

Put the buckle collar and leash on your dog. Hold the end of the leash with one hand, squat on the floor and offer your open palm with other hand, and give the command "Rover, come" in an upbeat voice. You want your dog to perceive that good things are going to happen when he comes to you. If the dog makes an advance toward you, praise him. If the dog freezes, bucks, or pulls away, stay where you are and ignore him. After he has settled down, place him in his exercise pen.

A variation on this technique is to have someone hold Rover by the collar. Walk to the end of leash, crouch, and beckon him to come. The holder must turn loose the dog's collar in sync with you saying, "Rover, come." If the dog hesitates, jerk lightly on the leash. If the dog comes to you, reward him with "good dog" and a treat. Practice these procedures a few times, and then try it later when the dog is not on leash.

Move the show outside. Practice first with the dog on leash and then off leash in a fenced yard. Crouch down and clap your hands or entice the reluctant pooch with a squeaky toy while giving the "come" command. Call your dog to "come" when you are about to offer him something he enjoys such as dinner or play.

When your dog is distracted and you have doubts about him responding, don't call him. Wait to call when success is more probable. If you need to summon your dog for procedures he perceives as unpleasant—pedicures or administering medication, perhaps—go and get him rather than giving the "come" command. Don't call your dog for punishment, either. Reserve "Rover, come" for occasions that can be reinforced positively.

What do you do if you give the command, and your dog doesn't come? You certainly don't continue calling and calling until you are hoarse and mad. Stop the training session, and start again next time at a previous level of competency. This might mean putting the dog back on leash or moving the training arena back inside.

Teaching "Sit"

The "sit" is a position that dogs use when resting their haunches while supporting their body with their front legs.

Attach your dog's buckle collar and leash and stand or crouch in front of him. Attract his attention upward by waving a squeaky toy above his head while saying "Rover, sit." Many dogs automatically sit if they are directed to look up. If your dog does so, praise him with "good dog" and give him a small treat.

An alternative method that might work for teaching some dogs to sit is shown in Figure 4.2; to use this method, give the sit command ("Rover, sit") as you gently lift up on your dog's leash while pressing down on his hindquarters. If the dog obeys, reinforce the behavior with praise and a treat. An occasional dog will automatically push back against your hand with this technique. If so, lift up on the leash while rubbing your hand over his back. Tuck your hand beneath his rump and apply pressure to mechanically encourage your dog to sit. Reinforce the sitting position with praise and a treat.

FIGURE 4.2
Urge your dog into the sit posture by lifting up on the leash while pressing down on the pup's rump, as you give the "sit" command.

After you've introduced sit at your regular training sessions, ask your dog to sit when he is highly motivated to obey you—before dinner and games. After the dog learns the frontal sit (you give the command facing him), teach him to "sit" while standing at your side.

GIVE A COMMAND ONLY ONCE

One of the most common training mistakes is repeating commands. Your dog soon learns that he doesn't have to react until you've repeated yourself the third or fourth time. Instead, teach your dog that you are going to give the command once. Solicit your dog's interest by showing him the tin containing his favorite treats. Give the command for sit. If the dog sits within a 30 second time limit, give him a treat. If not, turn your back and walk away. If he follows you, give him another chance to respond to "Rover, sit."

Do not give the treat until your dog correctly performs within the allotted time and work toward reducing that time limit. He will soon learn that failure to respond immediately will result in you leaving the room and in him losing the treat.

By the end of Week Two, you can hopefully combine "come" and "sit." Put your dog's collar and leash on and instruct him to come. When he obeys, say "good" and give him a tiny bite of treat. Then pull up gently on the leash while instructing him to sit. Reward the sitting position as shown in Figure 4.3. Work on phasing out the leash prompt and food rewards by using them intermittently and then not at all. Your ultimate goal is to have your dog "come" and "sit" in response to your verbal commands.

FIGURE 4.3
Call your dog's name followed by "come." When he obeys, give the command to "sit"; crouch to his level and praise him lavishly when he responds correctly.

Preventing Unwanted Puppy Chewing

Chewing is part of a puppy's normal exploratory behavior, and it relieves boredom; chewing soothes the gum irritation of teething and builds strong muscles and ligaments of the jaws and teeth.

> **note** Puppies aren't unique in exhibiting unwanted behavior. To learn how to stop other types of unwanted behaviors, such as jumping on furniture, begging at the table, digging in the yard, and so on, see the chapters in Part III, "Improving Your Dog's Manners."

The line between normal and destructive chewing is a subjective one. Chewing an old pair of slippers might be okay, but chewing the new Guccis is not. The problem is that most puppies can't tell the difference. If you don't want the puppy to chew shoes, prevent him access to all shoes. If chewing the drapery ties is forbidden, don't offer him a toy made of similar material.

Fetch

Provide the puppy with appropriate items to chew and praise him when he does so. If the puppy ignores your offerings, entice him by inserting peanut butter or freeze-dried liver inside a Kong or similar toy. Check out the Ruff-Puppy Teethers (to be placed in your freezer) for teething puppies at www.ruffdoggie.com.

Teach your puppy to play fetch with some of his toys (details found in Chapter 7, "Having Fun While Exercising"). If you see him chewing an inappropriate item, say "no" while the action is occurring. You might then divert his attention by throwing out a rubber toy for him to fetch.

Keeping the puppy in his exercise pen or crate (with acceptable chew toys) when you are unavailable to supervise prevents him from chewing destructively.

Curbing Puppy Biting Behavior

Teach your puppy to use his mouth gently and sparingly. If you are playing with the puppy and he bites you, immediately stop what you are doing and issue a sharp "no" (see Figure 4.4). If the puppy continues with his biting behavior, end the game by walking away. (This works best with the puppy confined to his exercise pen.) If the pup stops biting in response to your admonition, say "good dog" and continue the game.

Don't pull back if the pup grabs your pant legs with his teeth. Instead, admonish him with "no" and try diverting his attention away from you by throwing down a can filled with pennies or one of his toys. If this does not work, remove him to a separate room. Teach him that inappropriate use of his teeth will result in less not more attention from you.

Fetch

Certain puppies, retrievers in particular, will mouth or chew at their leashes. You can spray the leash with a bitter spray such as Grannick's Bitter Apple (available at pet stores) or wrap the leash in tin foil.

> **caution** Avoid playing tug-of-war games, wrestling, or play fighting with your puppy or dog. These activities teach him to use his teeth in an aggressive manner.

CHAPTER 4   **Manners Training: Week by Week**   61

FIGURE 4.4
Issue a sharp "no" as soon as the puppy misbehaves.

To do list

- ❏ Continue crate and toilet training
- ❏ Reinforce your dog's vocabulary
- ❏ Use the "come" and "sit" commands during daily interactions with your dog
- ❏ Train your dog to walk on a loose leash

Week Three: Introducing Leash Walking

The lessons we've discussed so far are suitable for any age dog. The exercises for teaching "come" and "sit" from Week Two can be now be incorporated into daily interactions with your dog. As you enter Week Three of your training program, ease off on the use of treats and ask your dog to perform for praise and petting only. In this week, add walking on a loose leash to your training routine.

Things You'll Need

- ❏ Your dog
- ❏ Buckle collar and leash
- ❏ Treats

Leash Walking Basics

Teaching your dog to walk politely on a loose leash is a more relaxed procedure than the more formal "heel" command to be introduced in Chapter 5, "Graduating to Next-Level Basics." Here you want to teach the dog to walk with you without pulling on the leash.

Choose an area for the walk where distractions such as squirrels or other dogs are few. Train in areas with more distractions after your dog has learned the procedure.

Attach your six-foot leash to the dog's buckle collar; place the dog on your left side (or right side if you are left handed); and start off in the direction of your walk while giving your command for walking. This command can be something like "Rover, walk" or "Rover, let's go." As soon as the dog pulls on the leash, stop and wait patiently until your dog turns toward you. As soon as he even looks in your direction, say "good" and offer him a treat. He should step toward you to get the treat.

Give the "walk" command and start off again with the leash loose, as shown in Figure 4.5. Keep the hand holding the leash at waist level and be careful that you don't take up slack in the leash.

If your dog is disobedient when you are working with him on leash, pop the leash and release it immediately while simultaneously telling him "no!"

> **tip** Give the dog the entire length of the six-foot leash whenever possible and make sure that the leash is loose by letting it swing. (The leash should be like a sagging rope.)

FIGURE 4.5
Walking on a loose leash is a fun way to explore the countryside with your dog.

Teaching Your Dog to Turn with You

The "turn and go" is a variation on the preceding technique. Start with the walk command and step forward. As soon as your dog puts tension on the leash, turn 180 degrees from the direction the dog is pulling, give your command again, and walk briskly in the new direction. When the dog turns to follow you, say "good" and offer him a treat. As long as he keeps slack in the leash, praise and reward. As soon as he begins to tighten the leash, turn and go in a new direction.

To do list

- ❑ Continue crate and toilet training
- ❑ Reinforce your dog's vocabulary
- ❑ Use the "come" and "sit" commands during daily interactions
- ❑ Practice walking on a loose leash
- ❑ Introduce the "down" command

Week Four: Adding the Down Command

If toilet training has progressed well to this point, make fresh water available at all times. Continue to use timed feedings and to leave the pup in his exercise pen or crate when you are not available to supervise. You can expand his territory to areas where you are working or socializing when you are home; however, attach his collar and leash so that you can bring him under immediate control.

Don't give in now to the temptation of lengthening the time spent in any one training session. Your puppy or dog will pay attention to and respond better by keeping the lesson less than 10–15 minutes (5 minutes for puppies).

Add to the number of daily sessions when you are home from work by interspersing play and/or exercise between lessons and by fitting training tasks into your daily routine. Reinforce "walking on a loose leash" while you and your dog travel to the neighborhood mailbox and practice "come" and "sit" before feeding or game playing.

Try to end training sessions on a positive note by issuing a command that you know your dog can obey. Now, you can legitimately reward him with praise and treats.

Things You'll Need

- ❏ Your dog
- ❏ Buckle collar and leash
- ❏ Treats

When your dog assumes the down position, he is essentially responding to your command with a submissive posture. This might prove challenging for certain dominant dogs. Teaching this position is important because it establishes your rank as pack leader and provides a means for disciplining your dog.

Start with your dog in the sitting position. Let him see the treat in your hand and then take the treat down to the floor while you say, "Rover, down." As shown in Figure 4.6, place your other hand gently on his shoulders to assist him in assuming the down position. Praise him when he lies down and give him the treat. Expect him to remain in the down position for only a few seconds, increasing the time gradually as he learns what's expected of him.

If your dog does not go down, position him by lifting his front legs and sliding them forward. Stay next to your dog to keep a hand on his shoulder to encourage him to stay down. Then, reward him for remaining in the down position and take your hand away from his shoulder as you say "okay" to alert him that he can get up. As training progresses, you should stop using your hand to cue the position. Rover should assume the down position in response to your verbal instructions.

CHAPTER 4 **Manners Training: Week by Week** 65

FIGURE 4.6
Entice your dog into the down position by offering a treat while giving the command and pushing him gently into position.

Some dogs will respond better with a favorite toy. Put your dog in the sitting position; then pat the floor in front of him with one hand while bringing the toy down and sliding it into a position on the floor in front of him and issuing the command. The reward for going down is the toy and praise.

It is up to you how formal you want the down position to be. The conventional down has your dog with his rear legs under him and his front legs extended. The relaxed down allows the dog to lean over on one hip. If you want your "Rover, down" command to mean the conventional position, reward him only when he lies in a proper fashion.

Be careful that you don't confuse your dog by combining commands. Don't use "Rover, sit down" or "Rover, lie down." The commands "sit" and "down" should be given and rewarded separately.

caution Don't suddenly jerk your dog's legs out from under him as this can frighten him, and don't manhandle him to make him stay down.

tip If your dog resists these exercises, tire him out first with exercise or play so that he's too pooped to put up much of a fuss.

To do list

- ❏ Continue earlier lessons
- ❏ Teach the "sit-stay" command
- ❏ Introduce the release word

Week Five: Introducing "Stay" and the Release Word

Use the "stay" command to keep your dog in a position such as "sit" and "down." Your dog should remain (stay) in these positions until you release him with a word such as "okay" or "free."

Like the feedback words "good" and "no," you can use the word "okay" or "free" for an immediate release without prefacing it with his name. Pick one word and use it exclusively for release. "Good" should be reserved for praising correct performance and not for releasing the sitting or down positions.

Things You'll Need

- ❏ Your dog
- ❏ Buckle collar and leash

Put the collar and leash on your dog; stand on his right side; and instruct him to sit. After he has been praised for sitting, bring the rings of his collar to the back of his neck between his ears. Fold the leash so that it is taut and hold in your left hand. Step in front of your dog and say "Rover, sta-a[a]y." Initially, you will remain in front of the dog for a few seconds before praising and petting. Release the command by saying "okay." Tap your dog on the shoulder to indicate that he can break the position when you give the release word. When your dog learns the release word, cease using the touch cue.

Each time you give the command to stay, remain in front of the dog a few seconds longer before rewarding and releasing. When your dog remains in the "sit-stay" for a couple

> **note** The three "D's" of obedience training are duration (the time you expect the dog to maintain the position), distance (how close you are to your dog when issuing the command), and distraction (what's going on around your dog). Each of the three "D's" adds a degree of difficulty to training. Introduce these one at a time. If, for instance, you ask your pet to "sit-stay" while the kids are playing nearby, stand next to him and release him after a very short time.

CHAPTER 4   Manners Training: Week by Week   **67**

of minutes, increase the distance you stand in front of him while issuing the command. Practice giving the command with your dog off leash and in different areas of the house or yard.

When the dog holds the stay position for five minutes with you six feet away, put him in the sit position, issue the stay command, and begin to walk slowly around him as illustrated in Figure 4.7. If the dog gets up to follow, immediately put him back into the sitting position in the original spot. Praise your dog as soon as he performs correctly, even if it is only for a couple of seconds. If your dog repeatedly breaks the stay, go back to a previous lesson such as having the dog "stay" for only a minute with you standing beside or in front of him in a distraction free environment.

tip Do not use treats held in your hand as a reward for teaching the "stay" command. Your dog will want to come to you for the treat. Reward instead with verbal praise and petting.

FIGURE 4.7
Teach your dog to stay while you walk around him.

To do list

- ❑ Continue earlier training
- ❑ Polish the "sit-stay" command
- ❑ Introduce the "down-stay"

Week Six: Teaching Your Dog to Remain in the "Down" Position

This week, we continue earlier training and add the "down-stay" command. By this time, you are probably asking, "How can I possibly teach my dog to sit, come, lie down, walk on a leash, and stay in position during one or two 5–15 minute training sessions per day?"

The answer is "you don't." By the time you reach Week Six, your dog should be coming, sitting, lying down, and walking on a leash in response to your commands during normal interactions with him or during a minute or two refresher lesson at the beginning of your training sessions.

note Teach each command initially in a distraction-free environment. After the lesson is learned, proof your dog by training in different circumstances and environments, and with different family members as trainer.

Things You'll Need

- ❑ Your dog
- ❑ Buckle collar and leash

Teaching the "Down-Stay"

Put your dog's collar and leash on him and stand on his right side facing the same direction. Give the command for down. If you are holding your dog in the down position by pressing on his shoulders, gently remove the pressure while saying "Rover, stay." If he "stays" for just a few seconds, give the release command (such as "okay") and show your approval with "good dog" and petting. If the dog breaks the position before you release him, gently place him back down in the same spot and repeat the procedure.

Increase the time you expect your dog to hold the down position with each successive training session until he will "stay" for at least five minutes. Then, give the "stay" command and begin moving around him. Shorten the time before release and gradually work up again. If your dog is well trained in the "sit-stay," he will readily accept the "down-stay" when you leave his side and increase your distance from him.

note Always release your dog when he is in the stay position before issuing another command such as "come."

Having Patience with Your Pet

Training Tip

It takes many weeks for the lessons presented in this chapter to gel in a dog's mind. If your dog fails to perform as you intend, assume that the problem is a lack of understanding on his part. Simplify what you ask of him and back up to an exercise your dog knows well. Then proceed in a series of smaller steps, using rewards to entice the dog to learn. Your dog might take 12 rather than 6 weeks to progress to "down-stay."

Summary

If your training has gone well, your dog now resides contentedly in his crate or dog house and eliminates on command in a location you have selected.

You have introduced him to come, sit, walk on a loose leash, lie down, and stay on cue. These obedience skills must be practiced throughout your dog's lifetime so that they are not lost. Providing your dog with ongoing leadership and guidance will ensure that your relationship remains healthy and happy. In the next chapter, we move on to the next-level training exercises, including heeling, more work with the "come" command, and giving some basic hand signals.

5

Graduating to Next-Level Basics

Training your dog is an ongoing task, and it is up to you to decide your teaching goals. This chapter presents a few more suggestions for training or for correcting emerging training problems.

Continuing with Recall and Leash Training

Allowing your dog to explore the outdoors off leash or taking him for a leisurely walk on leash might seem like an impossible dream when your dog has his own agenda. Provide direction and leadership by teaching him to "come" immediately when called and to walk politely at your side in response to the "heel" command.

In this chapter:

* Reinforcing your dog's response to "come"
* Teaching the "heel" command
* Using hand signals
* Adding clickers to your training régime

To do list

- ❏ Reinforce the off-leash "come" command
- ❏ Teach your dog to heel
- ❏ Correct leash problems

Things You'll Need

- ❏ Your dog
- ❏ Collars and leash
- ❏ Treats
- ❏ Cotton clothesline rope
- ❏ Head collar or no-pull harness

Another Technique for Teaching "Come"

We've discussed basic training methods for teaching your dog to come in the previous chapter, and you might feel reasonably sure that your dog understands the command. However, the pup who sticks with you at four months of age might suddenly develop his independence for exploring on his own when adolescence hits around six months of age. This is the time to reinforce the *recall*, another name for the "come" command.

Training your dog to come while off leash is one of the most important and, also, one of the most difficult lessons to teach. I know that I promised you a way of training your dog "in no time," and the basic process of teaching this behavior takes little time. But you must continue to practice and develop the behavior over an extended period of time. The following technique should extend over an eight-week period:

- Week 1–2: Cut off a 10-foot length of cotton rope and fasten a snap to one end and fashion a loop on the other. Have your dog on leash or rope when you go outside. Hold the line and walk away from the pup. Turn and call him using "Rover, come." If the dog starts toward you, praise him for any advancement he makes toward you. Drop down on one knee, and entice him by showing him a treat and repeating "good" when he progresses in the correct direction. Give him a petting or scratch and the treat when he arrives within reach. If the dog hesitates after you've given the first command for

CHAPTER 5   Graduating to Next-Level Basics

"come," give him a tug on the line. If he complies, praise with "good" and offer a treat. If he ignores you, reel him in with the rope. Reward him for coming to you even if he has no choice in the matter. Practice this technique two or three times daily for a week. If your dog is responding well, repeat this procedure in a new location (park, beach, front yard) or with distraction (neighborhood kids playing nearby, and so on) for six days the following week.

> **tip** Avoid teaching your dog that coming is the end of his pleasurable activity. If he's engaged in a fun pursuit, call him and then release after he does, so he can continue what he was doing. When it's time to end the fun and move inside, go get the dog rather than calling him to come to you.

- Week 3–4: Tie a snap on one end of a 30-foot rope (shorter for smaller dogs). Fasten the rope to your dog's buckle collar and let him drag the rope around the yard. Watch to make sure that he doesn't get the rope tangled around something and stay close to the end of the rope. Give the "come" command. If the dog fails to respond immediately, step on the line, and if necessary, pick it up and tug to get your dog's attention. Reward your pup for coming toward you. When your pup is responding reliably, add distractions and repeat the exercise in different locations.

> **caution** Do not allow your dog to run free in an open area until he's fully and reliably trained to come when called. Place him on leash whenever you take him close to busy highways. Consider enrolling your dog in a professional training course if you continue to have problems establishing this behavior in him.

- Week 5–6: Do not move to the next step until your dog is coming to you consistently and eagerly every time without you having to step on the rope. By this time, you should be offering the food reward randomly, perhaps every third time he responds. Continue to use a lot of praise and petting for correct recalls. Over the next couple of weeks, you are going to give your dog a new sense of freedom. Cut off two or three foot sections of the rope so that by the end of Week 6, the line is only six inches long. Practice in fenced outdoor areas.

- Week 7–8: Remove the rope, and practice the recall in outdoor fenced areas, moving on to safe, unfenced areas such as the school yard. Proof by adding distractions. Don't hesitate to back up to an earlier lesson when needed and to periodically give your dog a refresher course.

Teaching the "Heel" Command

The "heel" command instructs your dog to stand, sit, or walk at your left side. Teaching your dog to heel makes him follow your agenda, and not his, when you are out on walks together. If your dog is already accomplished in walking on a loose leash, teaching your dog to respond to "heel" should be easier.

note Obedience trial heeling is much more precise than the training techniques suggested here. If you are interested in perfecting heeling for competition, please refer to the many excellent books devoted to this topic.

Place the slip collar and leash on your dog and stand at his right side. Hold the leash in your right hand, folding the excess until you have only a few inches between you and your dog; stabilize the leash with your left hand as shown in Figure 5.1.

FIGURE 5.1
Hold the leash like this when working with the heel command.

Step forward on your left foot while giving the leash a quick tug. At the same time, give the command by saying "Rover, heel." As your dog starts off, praise with "good" and give him a treat.

Begin training by walking in a straight line using a brisk pace. As soon as you discern that your dog is lagging behind or getting ahead, change direction to the left

CHAPTER 5 Graduating to Next-Level Basics

while giving the "heel" command. Your dog's attention will be brought back to you as his collar tightens and you nudge him back into place with your left knee. Praise as soon as the dog assumes the correct position at your left side. Continue training by practicing left-hand circles, completing the exercise in the same position from which you began.

> **tip** It is easier to teach your dog to heel when using a rapid pace. You can reduce the speed once the dog has mastered the skill.

After your dog is heeling while going straight and making left turns, introduce a right turn. As you make the right turn, you might need to give the leash a quick tug while saying "Rover, heel." Be sure to praise as soon as your dog resumes the correct position.

Introduce the "heel" command during your regular and short training sessions and reinforce that training during daily walks. After your dog is heeling well, you can switch to the buckle collar and leash for your daily outings.

Formal heeling requires that your dog sit at your left side whenever you stop. You can add the automatic "sit" to your training sessions after your dog learns to consistently walk at your left side when traveling in any direction.

To do list

- ❑ Bring your dog to attention with a hand clap
- ❑ Combine verbal and hand signals for the heel, sit, come, stay, and down positions

Teaching Hand Signals

Hand signals are visual rather than vocal cues used for issuing commands. These signals help reinforce oral commands and aid in teaching your dog certain tricks. They may be used to convey your wishes to dogs that are deaf or becoming hard of hearing.

Training Tip

No official sign language exists for dogs. You can pick your own hand signals, or you can adopt the commonly used signals suggested in this chapter. In any event, however, the hand signals you select should remain constant throughout your dog's life, and the same signals—verbal and hand—should be employed by all family members.

HEAD COLLARS AND NO-PULL HARNESSES

Your hoped for relaxing walk becomes stressful and tiring if your dog pulls you along to explore each bush or to chase every critter in sight. Dogs that insist on being the leader when walking on leash must be corrected immediately and consistently. Head collars and no-pull harnesses are training aids suggested for rectifying this misbehavior. Figure 5.2 shows one example of a head collar.

FIGURE 5.2
A head collar is helpful for teaching proper leash behavior.

There are several brands of head collars, two of the most popular being the Gentle Leader and Halti. These training collars have two loops—one that fits around the dog's neck and another that goes around his muzzle; you attach the leash to a control ring at the bottom of the muzzle strap.

Many dogs pull back against pressure applied to the throat when you tug on a leash attached to a buckle or slip collar. The head collar, however, puts the pressure at the back of the dog's neck, closing the loop around his muzzle. This provides you with control similar to that of a pack leader encircling the nose and lower jaws of a subordinate canine or to a mother dog picking up a puppy by his scruff.

Fetch

Fitting collars snugly and correctly is very important. You should be able to slip only one finger under the portion of the collar that buckles or snaps behind the ears. The muzzle strap should not lay closer than a half inch to the eyes. On a Gentle Leader, the clip should be tightened up under the chin so that one finger fits under the muzzle strap. The Halti self adjusts under the dog's chin if you buy the correct size. You can review sizing instructions for the Gentle Leader head collar at www.gentleleader.com ([888]-640-8840) and the Halti at www.companyofanimals.co.uk.

Do not jerk or yank the leash when using head collars. Always use a gentle pull in your direction. If the dog attempts to lunge, quickly yet firmly take up the slight slack by lifting your hand upward and forward; then immediately release as he stops jerking and slows his pace. Reward with praise and a treat.

Gradually familiarize your dog to the head collar in a manner similar to that suggested in Chapter 4, "Manners Training: Week by Week," for introducing the buckle collar and leash. After the dog accepts the head collar as easily as his buckle collar, put it on him for a short walk.

No-pull harnesses are also designed to correct your dog's misbehavior or leash. See the Gentle Leader and Company of Animals websites for descriptions of and fitting instructions for their no-pull harnesses.

Things You'll Need

- ❏ Your dog
- ❏ Collars and leash
- ❏ Treats

Getting Your Dog's Attention by Clapping

When you are in a situation in which the noise level is high, a loud hand clap can serve to attract your dog's attention without you having to shout a command. When your dog hears the clap, he should immediately stop what he's doing, look at you, and wait for your instructions.

Place a few treats in your pocket, and invite your dog to join you while you work in the kitchen or read a book in the family room. When your dog's attention is focused elsewhere, stop what you are doing, look at your dog, and clap your hands. The clap should be a crisp, solitary one, not a series of claps. If he looks your way, say "good" and throw him a small goodie as a reward.

Resume your activity until your dog's attention wanders again. Clap once more, and reward him when his focus returns to you. Repeat, each time lengthening the time between the dog's response and the offering of the treat. This should serve to increase the time you hold his attention before issuing a command such as "come" or "sit." Practice outside as well as inside the house and with varying degrees of distractions going on around you.

Using Hand Signals for Heel, Come, Sit, Down, and Stay

Training with hand signals starts by combining your verbal command with the selected hand signal. After your dog learns the meaning of each hand signal, he should respond appropriately to either the verbal command or the hand cue.

Hand Signals for Heel

Prepare your dog with his collar and leash for his walk, and pick one of two signals typically used for the "heel" cue. The first is to simply slap your left leg with your left hand. You give the cue once and at the same time as the verbal command "Rover, heel." Then, off you go, leading with your left leg.

The second signal is to sweep your left hand in front of the dog's nose (do not touch him) at the same time you give the verbal command. Your palm should be sweeping in the direction you are going to be walking.

Hand Signals for Come

You might elect to just open your arms wide in a welcoming gesture while saying, "Rover, come." You can start by kneeling, opening your arms, and issuing the command. Progress to giving the signal standing.

Another signal to coincide with the "come" command is to stretch your arm straight out to the side, palm facing the dog. Bring your arm up toward your chest as you issue the verbal command as shown in Figure 5.3.

Hand Signal for Sit

Pretend you are holding a treat by bringing the thumb and first two fingers of your right hand together (if right handed) and pointing upward. Take the hand up in a vertical direction toward your chest while giving the verbal command.

Start training by actually holding a treat in that right hand. Hold your dog's leash in your left hand and stand in front of him. Take the treat from the direction of Rover's nose up toward your right shoulder while saying "Rover, sit." When he sits, praise and give him the treat.

Hand Signal for Down

Place your dog in the sit position while you kneel about two feet in front of him. Put your open hand, palm down, in front of you. Thrust your hand down toward the floor while saying "Rover, down." When the dog settles into position, praise and give him a treat. You can start by actually hitting the floor; eventually, you just make the motion without actually touching the floor.

Perform the same motion while on your feet. Practice in different areas of the house and then move training outside.

FIGURE 5.3
Stretch your right hand and arm straight out to your side at shoulder height. Bring your hand into your chest to indicate that you want your dog to come to you.

Hand Signal for Stay

Place your dog in the sit position and then give him the stay hand signal, which consists of you bringing the flat of your right hand, palm facing the dog, directly in front of you toward the dog's nose (don't make contact) while saying, "Rover, stay."

> **note** For an animated version of hand signals, visit http://www.malinut.com/do/signals.shtml.

The hand signal should be deliberate and last a full second, remaining motionless in front of your dog's face. Always release the stay position with "okay." Continue training with your dog in the "down-stay."

To do list

- ❏ Learn about event markers
- ❏ Practice using clickers
- ❏ Use clicker training for introducing nail trimming to your dog

Introducing Clickers and Other Event Markers

An *event marker* is a training aid, usually a noise like that produced with a clicker or whistle, which denotes the successful execution of a desired behavior. When training a deaf dog, the event marker can be visual—the light from a flashlight, perhaps.

As shown in Figure 5.4, a clicker is a small device that makes a clicking noise when you depress it. It offers the advantages of allowing you to precisely and consistently reinforce desired behaviors as soon as they occur.

FIGURE 5.4
A clicker is useful for training a dog to respond to obedience commands, perform tricks, and tolerate procedures such as bathing or nail trimming.

In Chapter 4, primary and secondary rewards are discussed. A click or light flash is a secondary reward. It has absolutely no value to the dog until you pair it with something like a food treat, petting, or toys that the dog wants (primary reward). After the clicking sound becomes paired with a primary reward, the click itself becomes reinforcing to the dog. The dog works hard to earn clicks, whistles, or flashes as they equal the rewards he craves.

Things You'll Need

- ❏ Your dog
- ❏ Treats
- ❏ Clicker
- ❏ Canine nail trimmer
- ❏ Cotton or gauze pads
- ❏ Nail file
- ❏ Styptic powder
- ❏ Wooden kitchen matches

Using a Clicker

The first step in using a clicker involves teaching your dog to associate the sound of the click with a forthcoming reward. In training terms, this is called *loading* or *charging* the clicker.

To start, gather a bonanza of treats. You'll use a lot of these, so go really small—about the size of an English pea. Keep the treats hidden in your lap, closed hand, or pouch so that the dog doesn't see them.

Click the clicker once and immediately give the dog a treat. Repeat until you've used up the entire pile of treats. Continue this exercise during your regular training sessions. By the end of the week, your dog should really perk up when he hears that click.

> **note** Visit www.clickertraining.com or call (800) 472-5425 for supplies, articles, and a list of trainers using clicker techniques.

> **caution** Don't abuse the clicker by letting the children play with it, and avoid clicking close to the dog's ear.

The next step is to use the clicker to denote desirable behavior. If you are teaching "sit," click the instant your dog's rump touches the floor, and then fork over a treat. The timing of the click is critical. If you are late, don't click. Wait until next time. Then catch your dog dropping into the correct position or lure him into the sitting position, click immediately, and give the treat.

Once the sitting behavior is learned, you add a gesture or vocal command at the beginning of the dog's desired action. Eventually, you can phase out both the reward and the clicker and ask the dog to perform in response to a verbal or hand cue.

I've presented only a bare bones introduction to clicker training. If you are interested in using this training aid, I suggest that you buy or borrow from your library several good books on the subject, including Karen Pryor's *Getting Started: Clicker Training for Dogs* and Melissa Alexander's *Click for Joy: The Clicker Training Answer Book*.

Using the Clicker to Introduce Nail Trimming

The following section about teaching a sensitive dog to accept pedicures is one example of using a clicker as a training aid. This method uses desensitization techniques (defined more fully in Chapter 9, "Eliminating Annoying Habits").

Load the clicker as discussed earlier in this section by teaching your dog that the sound of a click means a reward is coming. Then, present the pedicure in slow, progressive steps in a calm and positive manner. The dog, depending on size, can be standing, sitting, lying down, or cradled in your lap.

Begin by talking in a soothing tone as you accustom the dog for handling of his paws and nails. When your dog allows you to hold his paw, spread his toes apart, or expose a nail, click and offer a tiny treat. You might need an assistant if you don't seem to have enough hands to handle feet, clicker, and treats.

When your dog becomes anxious and pulls away, stop and wait for another training session. The dog quickly notices that he missed an opportunity for winning clicks and treats. Once he learns that handling his paws and nails brings clicks and treats, you can introduce the nail clipper.

A guillotine type nail clipper, such as the one in Figure 5.5, works well for small and medium-sized dogs. You might find that open-jaw clippers work better for large dogs. Allow the dog to see, smell, and hear the clippers as you activate them. When he sniffs, noses, or licks the clippers, click and reward.

FIGURE 5.5
Guillotine-style nail clippers work well for trimming some dog's nails.

After the dog has becomes acquainted with the clippers, put him in a comfortable position, and place a match stick next to a nail. You are going to clip the stick instead of the nail until your dog gets used to the sound of the procedure. Click and reward good behavior. Once you've managed to click and reward for snipping matches corresponding to each toe, you are ready to introduce the actual procedure during your next training session.

When your dog is relaxed, pick up his foot, expose that nail, and clip just the tip. Click and offer a treat. Proceed to next nail. Don't go overboard. If you've managed to trim, click, and reward for the nails on one foot, you are doing well. Save another foot for next time.

tip Keep your guillotine nail clippers in good shape by cleaning after use with alcohol and by replacing blades as soon as they become dull.

note Pedicare is especially important for the senior pet. As an animal reaches old age, his nails become soft and brittle, contributing to cracking and breaking. Frequent nail trimming will keep your older dog's nails in optimum condition.

CHAPTER 5   Graduating to Next-Level Basics

After your dog learns to accept nail trimming, introduce the scissors and nail file by the click and reward system. Complete the doggy pedicure by trimming the hair between the dog's toes and by filing rough nail edges.

The clicker is used here as a precise event marker for the behavior you want to reinforce. If you elect not to use a clicker, desensitize your dog to the nail trimming procedure by proceeding in tiny incremental steps, rewarding desired behavior with treats, petting, and the feedback word "good."

> **caution** During training, be extra vigilant to avoid clipping near the nail's quick. If bleeding does occur, hold a small piece of gauze sponge or cotton over the nail until bleeding stops. Commercial styptic or alum powder can be used to aid blood coagulation. Put a small amount on your gauze pad and hold it briefly over the cut nail edge. These supplies should be available in your pet first aid kit.

Summary

We've continued training presented in Chapter 4 by adding another technique for recalling your dog and for teaching him to heel. For those who need a little extra control over their leash-pulling dog, I've suggested using a head collar or no-pull harness before you develop "dog-walker's elbow."

Your dog should now come to attention in response to your hand clap, and your hand signals are a visual cue for him to assume certain basic obedience postures.

I've also given you a taste of clicker training, and hope that you will develop many delicious and ingenious ways for working with your dog using this click and reward system.

Training keeps your dog's mind sharp and his interest focused on pleasing you. Let's continue training in a fun way by perfecting a few basic tricks to be presented in the next chapter.

6

Having Fun with Simple Tricks

As anyone who has watched "Stupid Animal Tricks" on the David Letterman TV show can attest, the type of stunts that animals can learn to perform is limited only by imagination. But training your dogs to perform tricks isn't just an exercise in mild amusement. Both you and your pet benefit from the time you spend training and practicing a variety of commands. In this chapter, I will introduce methods for teaching simple tricks. Take these basic tenets and adapt them for teaching the tricks best suited for you and your dog.

When you choose tricks, consider your dog's aptitude for that specific stunt and your training abilities for teaching it. Most important, adhere to the premise of this chapter—make training fun for both you and your dog.

In this chapter:

* Learning the benefits of teaching tricks
* Choosing the right tricks for your dog
* Teaching your dog to communicate by ringing a bell
* Training your dog to roll over, bow, jump through hoops, and play dead

To do list

- ❏ Understand the benefits of teaching tricks
- ❏ Choose the right tricks for your dog

Teaching Your Dog Tricks

The training techniques for teaching tricks are much the same as those for teaching the obedience commands discussed in Chapters 4, "Manners Training: Week by Week," and 5, "Graduating to Next-Level Basics." For the most part, you proceed step by step and reward each stage until, eureka, your dog is ringing the doorbell when he needs to go outside to potty or playing dead to impress the visiting grandkids.

Considering the Benefits of Trick Training

Teaching tricks is a great way to spend stimulating time with your dog. He receives attention from you and gains the confidence that comes from performing well, as well as health-enhancing exercise. You, in turn, hone your people-to-dog communication skills and your training techniques.

Trick training will aid your progress in other areas of instruction. When your dog's attention lags during obedience training, introduce a fun task such as sitting up to beg. If your dog is a couch potato, get him outside to learn how to jump through a hoop.

Keep your dog interested in pleasing you by performing tricks rather than indulging in boredom-induced misbehavior such as digging in the yard.

Choosing the Right Tricks for Your Dog

Some dogs are better at certain tricks than others. Small, high-energy terriers might be more adept at feats such as jumping through hoops and "dancing" than a staid, squat bulldog. The bulldog, however, might take readily to rolling over and playing dead.

Retrievers are great at tricks that involve fetching and holding things in their mouths. The one dog I actually knew that could bring his owner a cold beer was a Labrador Retriever.

As discussed in Chapter 2, "What You Should Know About Training," one of the rules of training is "make it fair and fun." Don't ask your dog to do something that frightens him or is beyond his capabilities.

Capitalize on your dog's natural inclinations and fortuitous occurrences. If you catch Rover jumping, say "Rover, jump" and reward. In only a few practice sessions, he can be jumping on cue. It's a natural progression to shape the behavior from jump into "spin" or "dance."

Training for Bell Ringing

I once had a bear ring the doorbell at my mountain home. When I opened the door, the bear looked as surprised to see me as I was to see him. My visitor wasn't a trained bear. He had climbed my outside stairs and had inadvertently pressed the button beside the door with his big paw when he rose to peer in the door window.

Catching your dog ringing the doorbell accidentally like my bear and rewarding that behavior is one way to train him to repeat this action. Other methods are discussed in this section.

Things You'll Need

- ❏ Your dog
- ❏ Treats
- ❏ Bell or chime system

I know that some of you think that training your dog to ring a bell to go out (or in) is a dubious advantage. If your yard is unfenced, this is not the trick to teach your dog.

For others, though, stumbling to the door in your pajamas at the dog's ring and opening the door to a secure yard while you stay in a warm house is worth considering.

Several types of bells or chimes will work for training your dog to communicate via a bell. Much depends on your preference and your dog's physical attributes. Small dogs can learn to ring a desk bell sitting on the floor or a small bell attached to the facing or wall next to the door.

Larger dogs might use a series of Christmas-type bells affixed to a leather strap that hangs from the door knob, as shown in Figure 6.1. Training your dog to nose this bell rather than tap it with his paw serves to preserve the door's finish.

FIGURE 6.1
A series of bells make this system suitable for differently sized dogs residing in a household.

COMMERCIAL BELL OR CHIME SYSTEMS

For those interested in commercial products, check out the Pet Chime. This system consists of a portable, wireless radio frequency transmitter shaped like a paw print. When your dog depresses this plastic paw with his foot, a signal is sent to the receiver (chime) to summon you with a ding dong or dog bark. Transmitters are placed inside and/or outside your home while the receiver mounts on an inside wall or stands on a table. See www.lentek.com or call (888) 353-6835 for more information.

FIGURE 6.2
Your dog can signal you by pressing the Pet Chime paw-shaped transmitter.

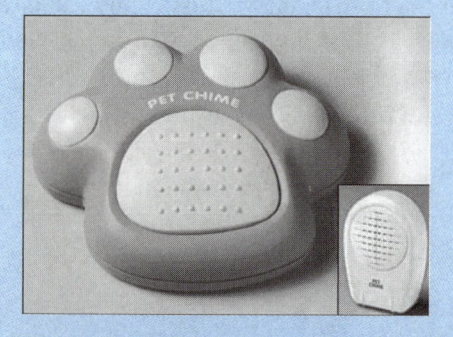

The Pet-2-Ring Doorbell works in a similar manner. Your pet strikes a push lever that acts as transmitter, the remote chime sounds, and you furnish the shoe leather to open or close the door for your pet. Visit www.pet2ring.com.

CHAPTER 6   **Having Fun with Simple Tricks**   **89**

Regardless of the bell system you rig, the training is much the same. Don't open the selected door in your pet's presence unless the bell is rung. When your dog noses or scratches at the door, take his paw and assist him in tapping or nosing the bell. After the bell sounds, open the door immediately and send him outside (or inside).

> **tip** Rub something with your pet's favorite scent (freeze-dried liver or peanut butter) on the bell to make it attractive to him.

Going outside or inside might be reward enough for your dog, especially if you give him the feedback word of "good." If he's used to a treat and/or click, use these training aids as well.

To do list

- ❏ Train your dog to roll over
- ❏ Teach your dog to bow
- ❏ Introduce hoop jumping
- ❏ Instruct your dog in playing dead

Selecting Fun Tricks

As I've mentioned earlier, the number of tricks that you can teach your dog is endless. Here's a few that might make your list.

Things You'll Need

- ❏ Your dog
- ❏ Buckle collar and leash
- ❏ Treats
- ❏ Clicker (if you've decided to use this method)
- ❏ Hoops

Teaching Roll Over

Bring your dog into the down position as taught earlier. With a treat in one hand, tell him "Rover, over" as you make a circle with the treat directly in front of his nose. With your other hand, gently turn him over. Roll in the same direction as you are signaling with the treat. After your dog learns the trick, you can tell him to roll over with a verbal command or with the hand signal—a circle in front of his nose.

Wowing with Bowing

Play with your dog, and when you catch him in the bowing posture (as shown in Figure 6.3), click immediately if you are using the clicker as an event marker and reward. Repeat until he responds to the verbal command "Rover, bow."

FIGURE 6.3
Reward your dog when you catch him in the bowing posture.

Training Tip: Here's another method for teaching this trick. Position yourself in front of your standing dog and hold a treat between his front legs. Once he starts to reach for the treat, move your hand slightly back, so the dog must now look between his legs. To keep his balance, he should now assume the bowing position. Say, "Rover, bow" and give the treat. To wow his audiences, have your dog take a bow after performing other tricks.

CHAPTER 6 **Having Fun with Simple Tricks**   91

Jumping Through Hoops

Fetch

Jumping through a hoop is a trick qualifying your terrier for the backyard circus. Appropriately sized hoops are available at craft and needlework stores, or you might use an old hula hoop found at a garage sale. Decorate your hoop to give a circus effect. See Figure 6.4 for an example.

FIGURE 6.4
Use an appropriately sized hoop for your dog.

Place the hoop on the floor and stand on the side opposite the dog. Guide your dog through the hoop with his leash and say "good" when he does so. An assistant holding the hoop might make the process easier.

Next time, give the command "Rover, up" while coaxing the dog with a treat. When he walks though on his own, give him the goodie. When the dog readily walks through the hoop, raise it a few inches from the floor. Reward the dog each time he walks through the raised hoop. After several training sessions, your dog should be jumping through a hoop that is elevated a couple of feet from the floor in response to the command "Rover, up."

tip If the dog attempts to walk around or under the hoop, move the hoop into position so he must go through it. If the dog manages to reach the other side without going through the hoop, withhold the reward.

Teaching "Play Dead"

My son-in-law Bubba taught my granddog Sarge many tricks, but my favorite was this one.

Bubba taught Sarge to play dead by teaching the following commands in progression: sit, down, over, and dead. This is a form of shaping.

> **note** Animal trainer Karen Pryor explains shaping in her classic book, *Don't Shoot The Dog! The New Art Of Teaching And Training*.

Shaping consists of taking a small tendency in the right direction and shifting it, one step at a time, toward an ultimate goal using a reward system. Bubba used pepperoni pizza toppings for positive reinforcement (reward).

When Sarge lays on his side in response to "over," Bubba says "bang" while pointing his cocked finger in the dog's direction. Sarge then lies flat on the floor as if dead.

Ultimately, the dog should "play dead" in response to one command—"bang" and/or the cocked finger signal and stay dead until released with "okay."

Summary

Develop a positive relationship with your dog by teaching him one or two tricks that are his special stunts. Pick tricks that build on behaviors that your dog does naturally or that are easy for him to learn.

The more behaviors you teach a dog, the quicker he becomes at learning new things. Once your dog grasps simple tricks, expand his trick repertoire to those requiring more comprehension to learn.

Having Fun While Exercising

7

In this chapter:
* Learning the benefits of canine exercise
* Choosing the right exercise for your dog
* Taking your dog hiking and camping
* Swimming lessons
* Teaching "fetch"
* Considering athletic competitions

One of the definitions *Webster's* puts forward for exercise is this: "activity for *training* or developing the body or mind." Using this definition, the lines between the suggestions presented in this chapter—such as hiking with your dog or teaching him to play fetch and the lessons that we've covered previously for house, obedience, and trick training—blur.

It makes sense to devise an exercise plan for your pet that engages both his body and mind. A sedentary dog residing in a crate, small room, or exercise pen during much of his day needs opportunities to run, play, and explore his environment. Without critical body work, his muscles weaken, his joints become stiff, his cardiovascular and pulmonary systems suffer, and he becomes bored and lethargic.

Take time now to choose activities that are suitable for your dog and commit to making them part of your daily schedule. Explore the exercise suggestions presented in this chapter or develop your own creative interests that will provide that critical form of stimulation for your pet that we call exercise.

To do list

- ❑ Take your dog to the vet for a checkup prior to initiating an exercise program
- ❑ Choose activities suitable for your dog
- ❑ Plan a gradual progression of physical activity to condition your dog for physical exertion
- ❑ Practice techniques for warming up before and cooling down after exercising your dog

Making Exercise Part of Your Dog's Routine

The benefits of exercise on human emotional and physical health are well known. Dogs, too, profit from exercise as active dogs are usually more alert, trimmer, and less stressed than sedentary ones.

Toning down an excitable, nervous dog or puppy with exercise makes your general obedience and house training go easier and smoother. Plus, many behavioral problems such as car chasing, destructive digging and chewing, and excessive barking are alleviated totally or in part when the misbehaving dog is given a vocation involving physical exercise. Your dog needs a job or activity that makes him feel useful and part of the family. If you don't assign him that job (performing an obedience command or fetching the newspaper, perhaps), he'll find one of his own, and you might or might not like his choice.

Interspersing your dog's exercise program with obedience work provides both physical and mental stimulation for your dog. The jog or walk around the lake is great, but make it more effective by practicing "sit" every fifteen minutes or so. Make the commands quick and snappy to keep the dog alert and thinking, and vary the place for and type of exercise to keep your dog interested.

Try to engage your dog in active play or exercise five or six days a week. When possible, incorporate your dog's activities into your daily exercise program. Ensure first that the pursuits you choose are suitable for your dog.

Things You'll Need

- ❑ Your dog
- ❑ Buckle collar and leash
- ❑ Treats
- ❑ Protection aids such as insecticide spray or sunscreen specific to your dog's individual needs and exercise pursuits

Choosing the Right Exercise for Your Dog

Consider your dog's breeding, age, medical problems, and physical condition when selecting physical activities.

The heavier a dog is in relation to his height, the more stress will be exerted on the musculoskeletal system when he runs or jumps. Taking your dog jogging with you makes sense if you own a Greyhound but is less of a good idea if your dog is an English Bulldog.

In some cases, physical stress is created by extra weight rather than breed conformation. Overweight dogs should be placed on a weight-reducing diet before attempting strenuous exercise.

Use caution when developing an exercise program for the very old or young. Refrain from taking your elderly pet on grueling expeditions, and delay activities such as long-distance trekking until a puppy's skeleton matures. The growth plates at the end of long bones close at approximately 10 months of age in small dogs and 14 months in larger breeds. Wait until puppies are past this vulnerable growth period before instituting extreme exercise routines.

Choose exercise activities well-matched with your dog's medical conditions. Dogs suffering from back and joint problems might not be suited to the running and jumping involved with Frisbee catching or agility trials. Yet, you can find activities that are suitable. Arthritic dogs benefit from non-weight bearing swimming and other water exercises.

note Take your dog to his veterinarian for a physical examination, vaccinations, and counseling about flea/tick control and heartworm preventative before choosing and starting an exercise regime.

tip White dogs are vulnerable to sunburn. Apply sun screen with SPF 15 or greater to thin-haired areas such as ear tips, nose, and groin when exercising outside at midday and at high altitudes.

Conditioning for Exercise

Take it slowly when introducing exercise to your dog, and monitor for signs of fatigue or pain. If walking is your pursuit, start out hiking only short distances. Increase the length of each trip gradually.

Be alert for signs of tiring such as changes in the speed or rhythm of your dog's gait. If you detect that he is fatigued, reduce speed and/or distance by one third next time.

Warm up and cool down after exercise. Moderately paced walking for 5 to 10 minutes is a good choice for warm ups in preparation for

caution Check for signs of distress such as overheating or sore feet. Dogs with pug nose conformation (brachiocephalic breeds such as the Boston Terrier) and obese dogs are especially prone to heatstroke. Take care when exerting these animals during periods of high temperature and humidity and avoid hot asphalt, which can cause blistering of tender foot pads.

more strenuous activities such as running or jumping exercises. Putting your dog through some of his obedience or trick routines such as "come", "bow", and "over" can serve as warm-ups.

Finish rigorous exercise with a cool down period. Use the same suggestions as for warm-ups. Water offered during cool down should be lukewarm rather than ice cold and given frequently in small amounts until the dog is cooled off and satiated.

To do list

- ❏ Accustom your dog to his backpack
- ❏ Accumulate supplies for hiking or backpacking

Hiking and Backpacking

A well-trained, friendly dog is one of the best hiking partners you can have along on your sojourn in the wilderness. I've hiked and backpacked with numerous dogs, ranging in size from a miniature Dachshund to a German Shepherd. All alerted us to intruders to our campsite and served as social magnets for introductions to others on the trail.

note When taking your dog from lower to higher elevations, go slowly and condition him (and yourself) to high altitudes before engaging in long or grueling hikes. Allow for extra rest periods and encourage your dog to drink copious amounts of water.

Almost any healthy, physically conditioned, and well-trained dog can accompany you when hiking or backpacking. The key here is "well trained." Dogs that routinely ignore your commands should be left at home until they learn the basics of obedience.

Things You'll Need

- ❏ Your dog
- ❏ Buckle collar, leash, and ID tag
- ❏ Canine backpack
- ❏ Collapsible water/feed bowl
- ❏ Poop bags
- ❏ Your dog's food, water, first aid kit
- ❏ Foam mattress pad or dog tent

Choosing Doggy Packs and Other Supplies

The only difference between a walk and a hike is the distance. If the distance is great enough, plan on spending the night on the trail by carrying your supplies in a pack.

You'll find that having your dog carry his own supplies is handy on day hikes and almost a necessity when backpacking. Select a well-fitting, sturdy pack and collapsible water/feed bowls, available at outdoor/pet stores.

> **tip** Your dog will be more comfortable in your tent at night with his own pad. Buy a small 1/2-inch closed-cell foam mat at Wal-Mart and cut an oval the size of your pooch. Or buy him his own Mutt Hutt tent (shown in Figure 7.1) from www.ruffwear.com.

FIGURE 7.1
A tent will protect your dog from the elements when camping overnight.

As a general rule, young or aged dogs should carry no more than 10–15 percent of their body weight, whereas healthy, conditioned dogs can usually manage 20–25 percent. During the training phase, strap on your dog's empty pack and let him get used to it at home. Engage him in a fun activity so that he forgets he's wearing a pack.

Next time, lightly load the pack and take off for a short hike. Make sure that weight is evenly distributed on both sides of the pack. Eventually, your dog should be able to carry his supplies including food, poop bags, first aid kit, and water bottle/bladder, as shown in Figure 7.2.

FIGURE 7.2
The author on the trail with her favorite hiking buddy.

Following Trail Etiquette

Even when you're in the "wild," your dog must be under your control. To keep you and your dog safe, and to avoid annoying other hikers and landowners, follow these basic rules of trail etiquette:

- Keep your dog on leash in heavily used areas and under verbal command while on the trail.
- Leash your dog around water sources and sensitive alpine areas. Do not allow your dog to stand in springs or other sources of drinking water.
- Give horses, mules, and llamas the right of way by moving your dog off the trail downhill.
- Do not allow your dog to chase wildlife.
- Leave no trace by burying your dog's waste as you would your own.

To do list

- ☐ Teach your dog to swim
- ☐ Accumulate the canine marine gear needed for your chosen water sport

Introducing Water Sports

Swimming and certain water activities are excellent exercise choices for aged dogs; those suffering from degenerative joint disease; and dogs fortunate enough to live close to rivers, lakes, and oceans. Some of these dogs take naturally to water, whereas others have to be trained or coaxed to get their feet wet.

Things You'll Need

- Your dog
- Buckle collar, leash, and ID tag
- Cooked hot dogs
- CD or cassette tapes with the sounds of running water and/or ocean waves
- Child's wading pool
- Canine life jacket

Teaching Your Dog to Swim

The first lesson is coaxing the dog into shallow water. You might take the leash and lead him in until his feet are wet, or you might encourage him to chase a rubber ball into the water.

If Rover's not buying your enticements, give him a bite of a cooked weenie before throwing the remainder into the water where the pieces will float on the surface. If food and play fail as incentives for getting your pooch into the water on your first visit to the lake or seashore, I suggest that you start over with the baby steps you would use to teach a young puppy.

Introduce your puppy to the sounds, taste, and feel of water. Play tapes of oceans and streams and run water in the sink to give an auditory presentation of water. Gently splatter a little water on the puppy's face. Fill a kiddie wading pool with a small amount of tepid water and entice the puppy to stick his feet in. Praise every step your pet takes toward accepting and playing in the water. If he becomes frightened, begin again at a later time.

When your puppy has progressed to the point of sitting and playing in the wading pool, it is time for an outing to the pool, lake, or ocean. Take care that the environment is free of distractions and dangers and that the weather is conducive to a carefree visit. Place a collar and leash on your pet, and let him explore his outdoor surroundings. On the next visit, he will be willing, perhaps, to get his feet damp.

Once your puppy feels confident about getting his paws wet, lead him into shallow water, taking care that he can touch bottom. Introduce a ball or other play item.

When your dog is comfortable playing in the water, pick him up and take him into deeper water. Support his weight so that he won't experience an unexpected dunking. As you release your hold, the puppy should begin paddling with his feet. Once the pet is actually swimming, move a couple of feet away from him while still holding his leash. Give him a command to "come." Reward each training step.

> **caution** Supervise all water excursions, and protect your dog from insects, animals, children, boats, sharp shells, and inclement weather. Get your dog out of the water immediately and dry him off if he becomes fatigued or cold. (Signs of distress include shivering and pale gums.)

Considering Life Jackets

Some dogs never become comfortable swimming in water over their heads. For these dogs and those with short legs and long backs such as Basset Hounds, consider a canine life jacket. Most jackets are constructed with flotation devices on both sides and straps/buckles to fit it to the dog (see Figure 7.3).

FIGURE 7.3
Ensure your dog's safety in the water by training him to wear a life vest.

Accustom the dog to wearing the device at home using distraction and reward. Then, introduce short, fun training sessions at the shallow end of the pool or lake. Move forward with subsequent training sessions until the vest-wearing dog is swimming on his own.

> **note** Visit PupGear at www.doggydocks.com for an array of marine-related pet products and www.ruffwear.com for the fitting guidelines/specifications about their K-9 Float Coat.

Playing Fetch

Anyone who has assisted someone during a building project can attest to the physical and mental exercise involved in fetching. Your dog will get in a lot of running time when you teach him to fetch; plus, he'll learn the words you use for different objects—hopefully better than I've learned the differences between socket, lug, and crescent wrenches.

Things You'll Need

- ❏ Your dog
- ❏ Buckle collar and long leash
- ❏ Treats
- ❏ Fetching objects

Teaching Your Dog to Fetch

To teach your dog to fetch, start with the object he likes most. Secure your dog with collar and long leash and place him in the sitting position. Release with "okay" as you toss the ball (if this is your fetching object) a short distance away. When the dog goes for the ball, give the command "Rover, fetch."

Once the dog has the ball in his mouth, tell him to "come." If your dog fails to return the ball, reinforce "come" by reeling him in with the leash. Then, trade a treat (the treat in this case could be food, another ball, or toy) for the ball, saying "good" when Rover releases the ball. Once your dog reliably brings the fetched object back to you, remove the leash and have him fetch the item. Encourage him to return it to you by excitedly saying, "Rover, come" while backing away and showing him the treat.

Once your dog is adept at fetching an object and returning it to you, teach him to drop it. Display a treat and give him the command "Rover, drop it" using your upbeat, excited voice. When your dog responds by dropping the ball, praise lavishly and give him the treat.

> **note** Pick fetching items that are a suitable fit for the size of your pet's mouth.

Some dogs are reluctant to release their fetched item. Don't play tug-of-war to get it. Try swapping another toy for it, or gently knock it out of his mouth while giving the command. Remember to reward as soon as the dog releases the object.

> **tip** The "drop it" command is useful for correcting destructive chewing or for alleviating potentially dangerous situations. Command your dog to "drop it" when you see him nuzzling your silk scarf or mouthing a toxic insect.

Once your dog grasps the concept of "fetch," teach him to retrieve objects by name. Work with one object at a time, and call it by the same name every time. If you want your dog to retrieve the newspaper, start by throwing a paper while giving the command "Rover, fetch paper." Reward only when the dog returns with the paper and drops it at your feet.

Considering Athletic Competitions

If training your dog for recreational physical activities has been fun, consider taking that training to another level by entering your dog in sporting events that will stimulate his mind and body. Competitions suitable for your consideration might include agility work, herding, hunting, retrieving, and field events.

Agility is a recently organized and fast growing sport. For agility titles, your dog must compete against other dogs of his size in a course set up with various obstacles such as tire jumps, tunnels, weave poles, seesaws, and teeter-totters (see Figure 7.4). As your dog's handler, you are given a set amount of time to direct your dog off leash through the obstacle course.

FIGURE 7.4
Balance and coordination are tested on the agility course's seesaw.

If you are interested in agility competitions, visit www.dogpatch.org/agility for links to agility articles, equipment, and classes. In the United States, several organizations sanction tests or trials that are set up by local dog training clubs. Visit the U.S. Dog Agility Association at www.usdaa.com or call (972) 487-2200 and peruse its offerings.

If your dog is a breed suitable for herding, hunting, or retrieving, consider training him for and entering him in the appropriate competition. Check out the American Kennel Club (www.AKC.org) and local and national breed clubs for more information. Ask for field trial rules and hunting tests applicable to your dog's breed.

The preceding are only a few of the more formal sporting competitions for trained dogs. Other fun events include flyball and Frisbee contests. If your sport isn't represented by an organization or contest, join your local training and breed clubs and start your own trials. Let the games begin!

Summary

Exercise is very important for mental and physical health. It works the body, expends excess energy, relieves stress, and sharpens the mind.

Let your dog's health, body type, and condition dictate exercise choices. Go slowly and use proven training methods for introducing exercise tasks. If your dog excels in certain sporting events, consider training him for and entering him in competitive trials. Most of all, have fun while exercising with your dog.

Part III

Improving Your Dog's Manners

8   Housetraining in Every Way **105**

9   Eliminating Annoying Habits **117**

10 Getting Tough About Serious Offenses .. **127**

8

Housetraining in Every Way

Does your dog think that he owns your home? Does he select a toilet, bed, or food of his choosing? Does he loiter on your favorite recliner, dig up your petunias, or steal your thawing T-bone? If you answered in the affirmative to any of these questions, pay particular attention to this chapter.

Discouraging Potty Accidents

In many cases, we contribute to our pet's bad behavior because we are so busy. We fail to take the pet outside on time or we fall short in reinforcing the toilet training lessons introduced in Chapter 4, "Manners Training: Week by Week."

In some instances, our pet's elimination problems stem from aging, as in the case of hormonal-related incontinence in older female dogs, prostate enlargement in males, cognitive dysfunction syndrome (canine senility), or other disease conditions.

Regardless of whether the problem is physical or behavioral, the longer we allow potty accidents to go unchecked, the more difficult they are to correct. Spend the time now to sleuth the cause of your pet's breakdown in housetraining and to take steps to rectify the situation.

In this chapter:

* Learning the causes of potty problems
* Retraining for proper toilet etiquette
* Protecting your furniture and other property
* Putting an end to begging and stealing
* Cleaning up your pet's eating and drinking habits
* Protecting your landscaping by nixing backyard digging

To do list

- ❑ Take your dog to the vet to rule out or to treat health problems contributing to your dog's potty lapses
- ❑ Retrain for proper toilet manners
- ❑ Put an end to submissive or excitement peeing
- ❑ Correct marking behavior

Things You'll Need

- ❑ Your dog
- ❑ Cleaning supplies
- ❑ Containment system such as baby gate
- ❑ Treats
- ❑ Medications prescribed by your veterinarian
- ❑ SleePee-Time Bed if your pet suffers from incontinence

Tracking Down and Treating the Cause

House soiling can result from medical conditions, inadequate training, excitement, submissiveness, territorial marking, and stress. Inappropriate elimination is often a component of separation anxiety (a topic covered in Chapter 10, "Getting Tough About Serious Offenses").

Dogs have an innate instinct for keeping their dens clean. If, however, the dog is forced to wait too long before being let outside or he has a physical condition such as a urinary infection or diarrhea, he might overcome his natural fastidiousness and eliminate in the house.

In some cases, what started as a physical problem becomes habit, and the dog continues to deposit urine or feces inappropriately long after his medical condition is cured. Initial steps in finding solutions for housebreaking problems include taking your dog to his veterinarian for a checkup and ruling out or treating physical problems that contribute to potty accidents.

note Distress in dogs can be triggered by unaccustomed changes such as a move to a new house, a visit from relatives, and a death in the family (animal or human). Dogs receiving inadequate socialization as puppies are especially vulnerable to this type of stress and might react with house soiling behavior.

Your veterinarian might prescribe drugs to treat physical conditions contributing to elimination problems. She might also prescribe medications to use in combination with behavioral modification techniques for curbing behaviors caused by stress. These medications include, but are not limited to, antibiotics for urinary tract infections, supplemental female hormones for incontinence, and tranquilizers and antidepressants for stress-induced conditions.

> **tip** Keep a daily log to ascertain the frequency, the circumstances, and the location of accidents involving urine or feces. This history will help your dog's veterinarian determine if your pet's elimination problems are physical or behavioral in origin.

Retraining

A recent Cornell University study showed that incomplete housebreaking was the predominant reason that owners sought counseling for canine elimination problems at the Veterinary Behavior Clinic.

> **note** Behavioral modification is defined as any of several techniques used to modify or correct a particular behavior. When you train your puppy to "sit-stay" on command instead of chasing the duck at the park, you've used a form of behavioral modification.

SLEEPEE-TIME BED

Pets suffering from intractable incontinence because of paralysis or other conditions might benefit from a product designed for "leaking" pets. This bed features removable fleece bolsters, a washable mesh bed, and a collection tray for urine. For more information, visit www.handicappedpets.com or call (603) 673-8854.

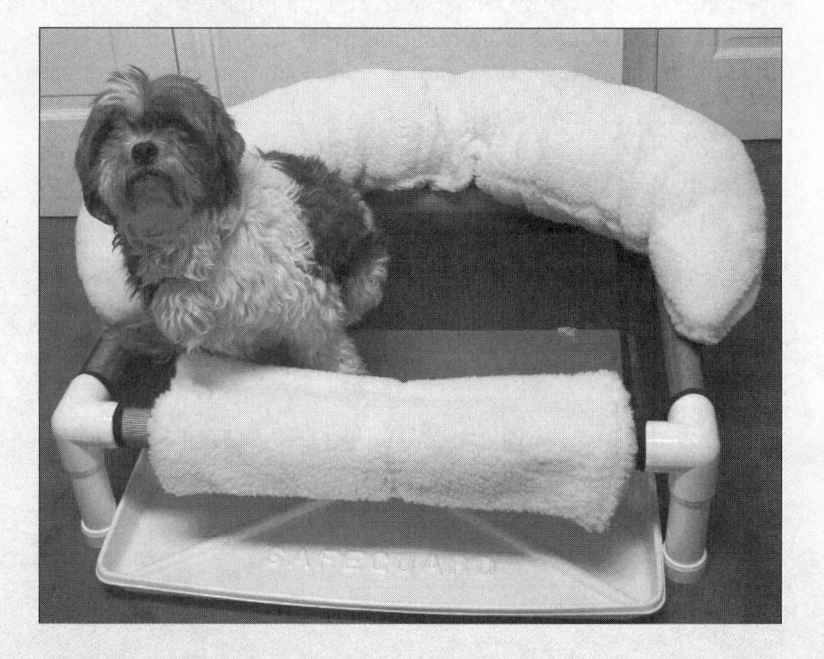

The solution for incomplete housebreaking—retraining—is simple but might not be easy. Please review suggestions for crate and potty training presented in Chapter 4. The following is a synopsis:

1. Thoroughly clean soiled areas, and where feasible, place the dog's bed or food bowl over the spot.
2. Reduce the dog's territory by use of baby gate or exercise pen. Extend his territory gradually when he proves trustworthy.
3. Reestablish a schedule for taking the dog to his designated toilet.
4. Praise and reward proper behavior and refrain from making a big deal about accidents.

Curbing Submissive and Excitement-Induced Urination

Certain dogs with subservient personalities might lie on their backs and pee, whereas others just sit or crouch and urinate as a sign of submissiveness. The act of urinating submissively begins early in a pup's life. After the mother nurses her puppies, she nudges them over onto their backs and licks them to prompt urination and defecation. Later, the mother merely looks at him, and the puppy rolls over or squats and urinates.

When an adult canine performs the same behavior, he is responding to dominant signals from his human parents. Dominant signals might include such innocent behavior on your part as walking toward, reaching for, leaning over, staring at, or speaking loudly to your dog.

During times of high excitement, dogs might dribble or squirt small amounts of urine. This behavior is more common in younger dogs, and many outgrow it in time. A stimulating event might be as innocuous as your return from work.

If your dog pees submissively or during excitement, take steps to decrease his level of arousal. When you get home from work, postpone greeting your dog. Do something else such as reading the mail or putting your coat up before addressing your dog. Have a long-lasting treat in your pocket, and toss it to the dog. Avoid looking directly in your dog's eyes, leaning over him, or touching him on the head, shoulder, or back, as these are often perceived as dominant gestures. Instead, squat down and rub or pat the dog's chest or under his chin when you pet him.

Maintain calm in action, voice, and environment, and avoid rousing the dog that pees during excitement.

> **caution** If the dog urinates in a submissive manner, ignore the behavior and clean up later. Avoid aggressive tactics such as shouting or hitting with a newspaper, as this will cause the dog to act even more submissive next time.

Putting an End to Marking Behavior

Urine and feces can be used to mark territory, provide a familiar smell, and to convey to other dogs the depositor's social rank and sexual responsiveness.

The presence of a new dog inside or outside the house might trigger your dog to assert his presence by urinating within his home domain. Although urine marking occurs more frequently in males, females occasionally use urine to scent mark. Males are more apt to deposit small quantities of urine on multiple vertical targets such as walls or draperies, whereas females are more likely to squat and urinate on horizontal surfaces.

> **note** In situations in which a dog feels anxious, depositing feces or urine on the owner's clothes and bed might be a way of covering a familiar scent with his own. This behavior is not meant for spite, but is an attempt by the dog to relieve the extreme anxiety he feels when separated from a beloved owner. See Chapter 10 for a discussion about separation anxiety.

If the dog chooses a particular spot to mark, clean this area of urine smell with an enzymatic cleaner (discussed in Chapter 3, "Getting Ready for Training") and make the marked area unavailable by limiting the dog's access or discourage the behavior with remote punishment (covered in the next section of this chapter). When a new pet is the inciting factor, take the steps outlined in Chapter 1, "What You Should Know About Your Dog," to reintroduce the new dog to your resident dog.

Because urine marking is most frequently seen in intact males, castration is the treatment of choice. The unwanted behavior should be eliminated within three months after surgery. Spaying females curbs heat-induced marking behavior. When neutering fails to remove the incentive to urine mark, your veterinarian might recommend drug therapy in addition to behavioral modification.

To do list

- ❏ Train your dog to stay off the furniture
- ❏ Correct stealing behavior
- ❏ Curb backyard digging

Teaching Your Dog Home and Garden Rules

You work hard to both pay for and to maintain your home as a safe and comfortable haven. Ensure that all family members, human and animal, respect your house rules for keeping it that way.

Things You'll Need

- ❏ Your dog
- ❏ Dog bed
- ❏ Treats
- ❏ Scat Mat
- ❏ Collar and leash
- ❏ Barrier fencing

Keeping Your Dog Off the Furniture

Some dogs like to be in an elevated position on the furniture to see out the window or to exert their social superiority. Others just like the feel of the comfy recliner or soft couch (see Figure 8.1). In some cases, this flexible surface feels better to their arthritic joints than the hard floor.

FIGURE 8.1
Banishing your pet from the couch becomes harder when he's laid claim to "his spot."

CHAPTER 8 Housetraining in Every Way **111**

If you started out making the furniture verboten to a new puppy or dog, your job of keeping Rover off the furniture goes much smoother. If your dog has already established the habit of furniture loitering or if someone in your family allows the dog access to the couch in your absence, your job of retraining your dog to stay off the furniture is going to be much more difficult.

First, you must provide a desirable place for your dog to sit or to lie down as an alternative to your furniture. Commercial pet beds are available in heated, orthopedic, designer, elevated models, and doggy sofa beds, to name a few creative categories.

> **caution** Allowing your dog to share your bed might signify (at least in the dog's mind) that he is equal to or higher in dominance than you. If your dog exhibits other signs of dominance such as rushing the door or crowding you off the sidewalk, reconsider this sleeping arrangement. When it's time for lights out, send the domineering pooch to his own crate, mat, bed, or rug.

You can make a pet bed from an egg-carton foam mattress cut to size and covered with a sheet or blanket. Or, you can continue to use the crate as the dog's place of rest and relaxation. Locate the bed or crate near family activity so that the dog continues to feel part of the family.

The technique for retraining is to lure the dog off the furniture with a treat and reward him by giving the treat when he gets off the furniture. If necessary, prompt him by pulling with the leash. During this step, take care that you don't trigger an aggressive response in your dog by startling him or getting right in his face.

You can also teach a command such as "Rover, off," rewarding the correct behavior with the feedback word "good" and the treat. Or, using positive reinforcement, you can train him to go to a certain spot with a cue such as "Rover, crate (bed or rug)." The "go to your rug" command is covered in Chapter 9, "Eliminating Annoying Habits."

If you see Rover ogling and approaching the couch, give him the feedback word "no." Say it in a forceful voice so that he gets the message. Until training is complete, avoid leaving the dog alone around the furniture. Close the door or gate off that section of the room.

If the dog has a preference for only one or two pieces of furniture, consider investing in a Scat Mat, available at pet stores, and placing it on items you are training the dog to avoid. The Scat Mat offers remote punishment by giving the pet a mild static electrical shock when he touches it. For more information, visit www.scatmat.com or call (800) 767-8658.

> **note** Remote punishment is designed so that the pet associates the negative event with the location of the misbehavior (the couch, for instance) or with the misbehavior itself (jumping on the couch) rather than the person administering the punishment.

Putting an End to Stealing

Does your dog steal the children's ball out of the toy box, the barbecue off the grill, or the leftover pimento cheese sandwich from the trash?

What is your pet's payoff for stealing? Do you wave your hands in the air and scream? Do the kids take up the pursuit for the toy? If the hoopla or the chase is rewarding to the dog, put an immediate stop to these games.

Training Tip

Be careful about punishing stealing behavior. If you catch your dog in the act of grabbing the object, you can command "no" or squirt with a water pistol. If you missed the actual event, refrain from reacting.

Deny access to the toy box, trash, or grill, and offer chew toys and puzzle boxes to keep your pet busy with his own toys. Check with your veterinarian about the quality and quantity of your pet's ration and his feeding schedule if he steals food. In some cases, the dog is hungry; in others, the motivation is boredom.

Ending the Yard Excavations

Dogs dig for numerous reasons—to make a cool resting place in summer, to cache and retrieve food, to investigate a critter hole, to excavate the garden or flower bed, or to escape the yard.

A bored dog digs more than one who has a job, so increasing your dog's activities with obedience training, tricks, and exercise are helpful preventatives.

Dogs that dig in flower and garden beds are lazy, I think, because it's easier to dig in loosely turned beds than hard-packed or grass-covered soil. To make these areas less attractive, set up a motion-sensor triggered water sprinkler or use a barrier system such as the Invisible Fence.

Rid your yard of moles and other critters enticing your dog to dig, and do not offer your dog items to bury.

Another method for preventing unwanted digging is to give the dog his own sandbox or digging mound. In this case, you use positive reinforcement each time he digs in his area.

> **note** *Fetch*
> For more information about the Invisible Fence, visit www.invisiblefence.com or call (800) 578-3647. This system consists of a remote transmitter that sends a signal to antennas buried around the perimeter of your property (or garden). When the dog, wearing a computer collar, approaches the boundary, the collar emits a warning beep, followed by a static shock if the dog crosses the border. The company offers dog training guidance.

THE "LEAVE IT" COMMAND

Use this command when you catch the dog in the "thinking" process of stealing (see Figure 8.2). Say "Rover, leave it" when he ogles or sniffs the hot dogs on the grill or the leftovers in the garbage can. During the teaching phase, consider setting up a training situation.

FIGURE 8.2
Give the command to "leave it" while the dog is contemplating a misdeed.

Attach a collar and leash to your dog so that you have control of his actions, and let him see the sandwich you've placed on the coffee table. When your dog approaches and shows interest in the bait, say "Rover, leave it!" If you give the command after he has it in his mouth, you've given the command too late.

If the dog continues to show interest in the food after you've instructed him to "leave it," give the leash a tug or pop. Say "good" when the dog looks at you instead of the bait or moves away.

Practice using different lures and surroundings and remove the item as soon as the training session has ended.

Broaden your use of "Rover, leave it" to tell your dog to ignore an approaching dog, passing squirrel, flying leaf, or toxic toad.

To do list

- ❏ Stop begging behavior
- ❏ Prevent drinking from the toilet
- ❏ Correct the ingesting of stool
- ❏ Have your dog checked for parasite infection
- ❏ Make the cat's litter box unavailable
- ❏ Administer food additives to render your dog's stool distasteful

Cleaning Up Your Dog's Eating and Drinking Habits

Dogs don't share our ideas about just what constitutes a balanced diet or an edible substance. Correct your dog's eating and drinking habits if they have become annoying, repugnant, or unhealthy.

Things You'll Need

- ❏ Your dog
- ❏ Buckle collar and leash
- ❏ Pooper scooper and fecal bags
- ❏ For-Bid or Dis-Taste Food Additives

Ceasing to Reward Begging

In his *Sniglets* cartoon, Rich Hall gives a great definition for canine begging: "the ability of a dog to inflict guilt from any angle in the room while he watches his master eat."

Resisting the canine begger is hard, and I've occasionally succumbed, offering a smidgen of snack to one of my trail buddies. This is called intermittent reinforcement—the reward, in this case a bite of food, occurs sporadically. The dog never knows when I might relent and give up my string cheese or power bar, and therefore, gives me that pleading look each time I pop food in my mouth in his presence.

If you and I want to stop this behavior, the correct tactic is to ignore begging when it occurs and to *never* give in. This requires commitment from all family members, as everyone must hang together to extinguish begging behavior (see Figure 8.3).

FIGURE 8.3
It's hard to resist those pleading eyes, but you must not give in to begging behavior.

The best policy is to offer your dog high-quality dog food once or twice a day, in his own bowl located away from the family dining area. You can also make your dining room off-limits to the dog or command him to "sit-stay" or "down-stay" in a location of your choosing (see Chapter 4).

Even after the dog appears to stop begging, he might suddenly take it up again. Continue to ignore the behavior, and it will go away much faster this time when the dog realizes that you are not going to give in.

Preventing Toilet Drinking

When a dog is thirsty, he'll drink from whatever is available, including the porcelain throne. Other dogs seem to prefer toilet water, regardless of the various fresh water sources you provide.

Drinking from the toilet can be hazardous to your dog's health. Drop-in cleaning tablets are corrosive to the intestinal tract when ingested. Commodes in cold-climate vacation homes and recreational vehicles treated with antifreeze are potentially a source of poison.

The answer to preventing toilet drinking is obvious—put down the lid or close the bathroom door. The hard part is ensuring that all family members follow this rule.

Closing the Poop Buffet

Although the thought of ingesting feces is repugnant to us, it is normal canine behavior for a mother dog to keep her nest clean by ingesting puppies' feces and urine.

Dogs that indulge in *coprophagia*, the scientific term for this behavior, might ingest their own stool or that of other animals. When the dog eats the feces of other dogs and cats, he increases his exposure to parasites.

tip If your dog ingests the stool of other dogs or cats, consult your pet's veterinarian about internal parasite control.

Ways to deal with this behavior include walking the dog on leash and removing feces as soon as it is deposited, as well as training the dog to defecate on command or to return to the home immediately after eliminating.

For-Bid and Dis-Taste, available in powder or tablet form at pet stores/veterinary clinics, render the stool of the animal ingesting the additive unpalatable. If your dog consumes his own stool, you add the drug to his food; if he ingests the cat's stool, you must add it to the cat's food. These drugs only work when given. As soon as you stop doctoring the food, the dog resumes eating poop.

If the dog is attracted to the fecal deposits in the cat's litter box, the remedy is to find a creative location for the box that will allow the cat access but not the dog.

Summary

Learning the motivation behind your pet's destructive house and yard habits is the first step in devising a correction. Take action to ease any health issues that are contributing factors and make sure that you aren't sabotaging your pet's training by giving in to behaviors such as begging or inadvertently rewarding attention-seeking tactics such as stealing.

Repeat training lessons when lapses occur and incorporate new commands such as "leave it" and "off" as situations demand. Doggy proof your house by declaring certain areas off-limits, and continue to provide your dog with guidance, rewarding good canine behavior while using behavioral modification techniques to curb those you want to extinguish.

9

Eliminating Annoying Habits

In this chapter:
* Silencing the barker
* Stopping your dog from jumping up on people
* Turning off door rushing
* Bringing a halt to crotch sniffing and restraining the sexual exhibitionist

There's nothing like hosting the PTA and having your dog jump up on guests with his dirty paws or hump the sofa cushion as you are serving refreshments to tell you that "something's got to be done." If you've been living with a dog with embarrassing or irritating behavior, take heart. Annoying canine habits can be changed or corrected.

Silencing Excessive Vocalizations

Dog Speak

Barking (and howling, growling, yelping, whimpering, whining, and moaning) are all part of a dog's normal communication repertoire. Dogs vocalize to greet others, to sound the alarm, during play, in defense, to define territory, during distress, to alleviate boredom, and to gain attention. See Table 9.1 for a meaning behind the various sounds that canines use for communication.

To do list

- ❏ Stop barking payoffs
- ❏ Teach the "quiet" command
- ❏ Deny access to or desensitize to situations in which your dog barks excessively
- ❏ Distract or use remote punishment for correction
- ❏ Investigate bark collars

Table 9.1 Canine Vocal Communication

Vocalization	Meaning
Bark	Warning, greeting, attention seeking, excitement
Howl or bay	Assemble pack, greeting, alarm, location marker, celebration
Growl	Threat, play (teeth hidden)
Yelp	Pain
Cry or whimper	Fright, pain
Whine	Attention seeking
Moan	Pain, pleasure

Things You'll Need

- ❏ Your dog
- ❏ Treats
- ❏ Water pistol, rattle can, or other method for disrupting barking
- ❏ Bark collar

Dealing with Excessive Barking, Howling, or Whining

Discovering the reason that a dog vocalizes is important in implementing the proper assistance or correction.

If your dog started barking or howling excessively in his golden years, deafness might be the reason. Older dogs with waning senses of sight, hearing, touch, and smell might feel isolated, particularly at night. Take special care to reassure your dog before you send him to his bed, and leave on a night light to illuminate the way to his water bowl and indoor toilet or doggy door.

CHAPTER 9   Eliminating Annoying Habits

Puppies often whine, especially when you and the kids leave for work and school. If you rush to pick up the puppy while saying, "Oh, my poor baby," you are reinforcing the behavior.

Better to ignore the protestations and reward silence with attention. This goes for any age dog. Only pet your dog when he is silent. Each time the dog is quiet when he would normally have barked, praise him and give a treat. Add the "quiet" command to your training schedule. If your dog is barking, tell him "no." If he doesn't stop, tap him lightly on the nose and say "Rover, quiet." If he stops barking, gave him a feedback of "good" and a treat.

> **caution** If barking or howling is accompanied by panting, salivation, restlessness, or excessive activity, the dog might be suffering from separation anxiety, a more serious behavior addressed in Chapter 10, "Getting Tough About Serious Offenses."

Does your dog pollute the neighborhood with noise primarily when the family is away? You might need to stage a leave taking and sneak back to spy on your dog to find out. Or, you can set up a videotape recorder to note the evidence.

Some dogs seem to bark at anything and everything, whereas others are more discerning. If your dog barks at what he perceives as intruders into his territory, as shown in Figure 9.1, obstruct his visual and hearing access to passersby on the street. This might mean drawing the drapes for indoor dogs and adding solid panels to your chain-length fence for outdoor dogs.

FIGURE 9.1
The dog barks, the postmistress leaves, and the dog perceives that he has chased her away. Socialize the dog to view strangers as non-threatening or block his access to them.

DESENSITIZATION

Desensitization is the process of training an animal to be less sensitive or reactive to a stimulus. This behavioral modification technique works well for treating fears or phobias (described in Chapter 10) and learned behaviors such as barking at the ringing telephone.

The following is suggested for the dog who barks at ringing telephones. Switch the ringer off until you are present to supervise. When you are available for training, turn the ringer amplification to low and distract the dog with petting or play when the phone rings. (Have an assistant help with the calling.) Gradually, over a period of days and weeks, increase the frequency and volume of the telephone ring until it fails to elicit the dog's usual barking behavior.

Correcting with Distraction and Punishment

Distracting the dog from barking can be as simple as yelling "no" or shaking a can filled with pennies. Once the dog is distracted, redirect his attention to obeying an obedience command or performing a trick.

Sometimes it's hard to discriminate between distraction and remote punishment. Squirting the indoor barker with a water pistol or the outdoor dog with a hose when he begins barking distracts as well as punishes. If your dog perceives the squirting water as a new game, find another means of distracting and/or punishing.

BARK COLLARS

Sonic and ultrasonic bark collars emit high-frequency, unpleasant (to the dog) sounds to disrupt and punish the barking dog. These collars are triggered in one of two ways: The collar emits a sound when activated by a remote transmitter controlled by you, or the collar releases its sound in response to a bark-activated speaker located on the collar.

The shock bark collar administers an electric shock of variable and settable intensity. Models are activated in the two ways similar to the preceding sound models. Some automatic types come with a shut-off feature. If the dog continues barking, the unit shuts down.

The citronella bark collar releases a harmless but disagreeable spray of citronella from a canister worn on the collar in response to barking. Studies show that this kind of collar works best when worn by the dog intermittently instead of continuously. Citronella collars are reputed to be more effective in curbing excessive vocalization than either the shock or ultrasonic sound collars; however, you must purchase citronella refills, and this can become an expensive drawback.

CHAPTER 9   **Eliminating Annoying Habits**   **121**

Bark collars are not a magic solution to excessive barking, and not every dog responds satisfactorily. Because the shock collar works by punishing through pain and can make aggressive behavior and anxiety-induced conditions worse, use only under the direction of a professional dog trainer, behavioral consultant, or veterinary behaviorist. See Appendix A, "References and Resources," for recommendations for finding professional assistance.

To do list

- ❏ Remove attention and rewards for jumping up
- ❏ Teach your dog to sit when greeting people
- ❏ Correct jumping up behavior

Putting a Stop to Jumping Up

When we lived in the city, my dog Bear had the annoying habit of jumping up on me when I went into his territory, the backyard. He ceased jumping up when we moved to our rural home in the mountains. In our case, the move to an interesting and stimulating environment took care of the problem.

Dog Speak

Jumping up and licking behavior might have originated from wolves, who lick each other on the face in greeting. Like Bear, some dogs jump up for attention and during times of excitement. For others, it might be a display of dominance (see Figure 9.2).

Things You'll Need

- ❏ Your dog
- ❏ Treats
- ❏ Slip or head collar and leash

Making Corrections

If you interact with your dog when he is jumping up, you have reinforced this action. Even pushing the dog away and yelling serves to give the dog attention. Instead, remove all rewards for jumping behavior. Turn away and then give a command such as "sit." Reward the sitting behavior with attention, praise, and perhaps a treat.

FIGURE 9.2
Jumping up and licking you in greeting may be cute when your dog is a puppy but becomes annoying and unsafe when he grows into a 200-pound adult.

Train your dog that sitting is the proper position for greeting. When you and your dog are out for walk and see your neighbor, ask your neighbor to refrain from greeting or petting your dog until you've put him into a sitting position.

You can also use a slip or head collar and leash to give you more control in curbing your dog's enthusiasm. If Rover starts jumping up on you or your neighbor, give the leash a tug as you give the verbal correction of "no!" Repeat the command for sit, and reward that behavior.

To do list

- ❑ Teach your dog to wait for you to enter first and give permission before he proceeds through a gate or door
- ❑ Train your dog to go to his rug or mat when the doorbell rings

CHAPTER 9   Eliminating Annoying Habits

Putting a Stop to Gate and Door Rushing

Does the door bell elicit a contest between you and your dog to see who can dash there the fastest? Does your dog bark and jump with excitement, nearly bowling visitors over with his enthusiasm when you open the door? Is he the first one through the door or gate when you are together? If so, you need to put an instant stop to this misbehavior.

Things You'll Need

- ❑ Your dog
- ❑ Buckle collar and leash
- ❑ Treats
- ❑ Rug or mat

Ending Pushy Behavior at Doors and Gates

Going through the door or gate first is a sign of dominance. Teach your dog that he should wait at entryways and let you proceed ahead of him. As shown in Figure 9.3, train your dog to "sit-stay" at doors and gates. He should remain in position until you release him to go through with "okay."

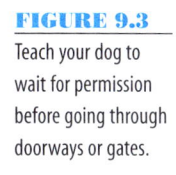

FIGURE 9.3
Teach your dog to wait for permission before going through doorways or gates.

Place Rover on a leash and lead him to within a few feet of the doorway or gate. Command him to sit and then to stay. Walk through the doorway or gate. If Rover dashes forward, correct him with "no!" Start again by returning him to the spot where you left him. If he breaks the stay again, give the leash a snap as you say "no."

> **tip** Don't chase your dog if he goes through the gate before you, as he might perceive this as a game

When your dog learns to hold the stay at doors and gates, go through the entrance, turn back, and release Rover with "okay." Reward him with praise and a treat.

Teaching Proper Doorbell Etiquette

You can control the canine door rusher by training him to perform an incompatible behavior. The behavior might be a sit-stay as mentioned earlier or a new command such as "Rover, rug."

Our goal in the last example is to teach the dog to respond to a ringing doorbell (or knock) by going to his rug, mat, blanket, or a specific spot, lying down, and staying until you release him (see Figure 9.4).

FIGURE 9.4
Teach your dog to lie quietly on his rug instead of rushing the door.

It is easier to teach your dog doorbell etiquette if you start training before the doorbell rings with an authentic visitor. Pick a spot near the door, but out of the line of traffic, and make this target obvious by using a rug or mat.

Place a treat on the rug so that the dog can see it. With your dog on leash, walk him to within five steps of the rug. Say "Rover, rug" and let him have the treat. If he doesn't approach the rug, lead him over to it, repeat the command, and then give him the treat. Practice this scenario until your dog consistently moves to his rug in response to "Rover, rug."

The next step is to put your dog into the down-stay position on the rug, rewarding again for correct performance. Remember to release the stay. Once your dog is consistent in holding his position on the rug until released, you can add the sound of the doorbell. Recruit a family member to ring the doorbell (or use a remote controlled device). When the doorbell rings, give the command "Rover, rug" and reward. Eventually you will phase out the verbal command so that the doorbell becomes the cue for the "go to the rug" response.

The final step is to teach the dog that he will receive attention, praise, and treats if he remains quietly on his rug when visitors enter the house. Practice with friends who are willing to follow your instructions for greeting the dog.

> **tip** It's okay to ask those who ring your doorbell to wait while you send your dog to his rug before opening the door. Request that all guests refrain from petting or interacting in any way with the dog unless he is holding the "stay" position on his rug. Keep a jar of goodies near the door for callers to reward the dog for good behavior.

To do list

- ☐ Put an end to crotch sniffing
- ☐ Neuter an intact dog to stop mounting behavior
- ☐ Assert your role as top dog
- ☐ Remove the incentive for your dog to hump by withdrawing attention

What to Do When Your Dog Gets Personal

Crotch sniffing and mounting behavior by your dog usually elicits a response from you and others. If the dog is performing for attention, the prize is your horrified reaction. Mounting might also be sexually motivated, a display of dominance, an attention-seeking behavior, and rarely, a sort of obsessive/compulsive disorder.

Things You'll Need

- ☐ Your dog
- ☐ Head collar and leash

Ending Nose-to-Crotch Sniffing

Dog Speak

As discussed in Chapter 1, "What You Should Know About Your Dog," dogs greet each other by smelling the inguinal area (crotch) and anus of other dogs. When your dog noses under a visitor's skirt or smells another's crotch, he's doing what comes naturally.

If you or your guest retreats in horror when you get cold nosed by a canine, he might interpret this withdrawal as submissiveness on your part. Make the dog back away by moving boldly and bodily into him while sharply admonishing with "no!" Diverting the dog's attention or bringing him under an obedience command will rescue the visitor being sniffed up.

Putting an End to Mounting

Although mounting or humping is considered a sexual action, it can also be used to signal superior social rank of male and female dogs. Mounting is also an extension of puppy play behavior, and a young dog will often outgrow it.

> **note** In some cases, your veterinarian might prescribe medications to help curb your pet's libido and dominance traits while you employ behavioral modification training at home.

Because mounting and masturbation are more likely to occur in intact males, castration is the recommended treatment. Occasionally, a neutered male or female will continue to engage in this behavior, leading me to believe that there is a learned component as well as memory of pleasure in some of these dogs.

Mounting is more likely to occur in dogs with dominance tendencies; therefore, take steps to both distance yourself from and to assert your leadership role in your relationship with your dog. Remove the dog from your bedroom, and make him work by performing an obedience command before you pet or interact with him in any way. A head collar might be indicated for controlling your dog and correcting him when he starts humping behavior.

Summary

Dogs are social animals, and many of the behaviors that are normal within the animal kingdom are irritating to people who have become their dog's social cohorts.

You do not have to live with your dog's embarrassing or annoying habits. To devise effective and healthy corrections, it helps to know your pet's motivation for his barking, jumping up, rushing the door, or sexual exhibitionism.

If your dog is excitable, keep his stimulation to a minimum. Remove his pay-offs for attention-seeking behavior. Maintain your position as leader of his social pack if he shows dominance behavior, and provide reassurance and a calm environment for those dogs prone to anxiety. Take your dog to his veterinarian for neutering or medical treatments for physical conditions contributing to his misbehavior.

In the next chapter, you learn how to curb aggression and fighting behavior in dogs, as well as how to avoid problems associated with predatory behavior, separation anxiety, and phobias.

10

Getting Tough About Serious Offenses

Domesticated dogs are most likely the descendants of wolves, and many behaviors such as aggression and chasing prey are reflections of this wild ancestry. In other instances, fear becomes the overriding emotion causing our pet dogs to exhibit extreme reactions to their environment in the form of phobias or separation anxiety. Regardless, these behaviors often become disconcerting, and in many cases destructive and dangerous. This chapter is devoted to a discussion of serious offenses, as well as steps for curbing them.

Putting a Stop to Aggression

Aggression is a threat or harmful deed directed toward another living being. Aggression toward people, particularly family members, is the primary reason that dogs are presented to veterinary behavioral services for treatment.

In this chapter:

* Learning the causes of canine aggression
* Taking steps to prevent or correct aggressive behavior
* Curbing predatory behavior
* Soothing your pet's separation anxiety
* Understanding and treating your dog's phobias

To do list

- Continue to socialize your dog to people and other animals
- Practice obedience commands
- Use the "no free lunch" approach for interactions with your dog
- Document aggressive misbehavior
- Develop a list of professional dog trainers and animal behaviorists to call for assistance
- Teach all family members to protect themselves against dog bites
- Make sure that your homeowner's insurance offers adequate liability protection for owning a dog

A dog might act aggressive toward others because he is

- expressing dominant traits
- possessive of objects, including food and toys
- guarding his perceived territory
- reacting to fear or pain
- protecting puppies
- redirecting animosity during play
- engaged in hunting behavior
- suffering from certain medical conditions

note A determination of aggressive type is usually necessary before a treatment regime can be recommended or a prognosis given. When your dog's behavior becomes potentially dangerous to others, consult with a behavioral expert. See Appendix A, "References and Resources," for a source of behavioral consultants and suggestions for choosing the right behaviorist or trainer for your dog.

Diagnosing a dog as overly aggressive is like saying he suffers from cancer. There are many forms of cancer warranting many different approaches to therapy, and so it is with aggressive misbehavior.

Things You'll Need

- Your dog
- Head collar and leash
- Water hose, citronella spray, or other means of distracting
- Basket muzzle
- Copy of your homeowner's insurance policy

WHAT AN ANIMAL BEHAVIORIST WANTS TO KNOW

Before consulting with a trainer or animal behaviorist, document your answers to the following questions:

1. What is the age, sex (intact or neutered), and general health of your pet?
2. Which people and animals reside in your home?
3. Does your dog bark at, growl at, or bite others? Are these behaviors directed at people, other dogs, or animals other than dogs? When, how often, and under what circumstances?
4. Has your dog ever bitten anyone? If yes, give your reasons for thinking that the behavior was accidental, deliberate, the dog's fault, or not the dog's fault.
5. Has anyone expressed the sentiment that he was afraid of your dog? If so, what are his reasons for this fear?
6. Is your dog showing signs of other behavioral problems? If yes, what, when, where, and under what circumstances.

Incorporating Tough Love for the Dominant Pooch

Because of conventional pack attitude, dogs push toward the highest position that they can achieve within their social circle, which includes family members and other dogs.

You might find that the dominant dog is aggressive to one or all family members, although typically he will choose those closest to him in status within the family pack or those he perceives as challenging him. He is less likely to confront family members who are clearly dominant or clearly submissive.

Aggressive signs such as growling, snapping, or biting are often perceived by family members as unpredictable or unprovoked. If you closely observe the dog's conduct, however, you might notice that one or more of these behaviors is a reaction to certain interactions with your pet.

> **note** Specific drugs are prescribed by veterinarians for identifiable conditions after an accurate diagnosis has been ascertained. If drug therapy is part of your veterinarian's treatment regime, it is usually short lived. Lasting behavioral changes are achieved by clear, consistent leadership on your part and by behavioral modification, including training of obedience commands and by incorporating the "no free lunch" program into daily interactions with your dog.

Dominance-related aggression might occur during the following events:

- The dog is disturbed while resting, sleeping, playing, or protecting a coveted object or person.
- The dog is being restrained, pulled on a leash, disciplined, groomed, medicated, or lifted.
- The dog is being petted, hugged, stared at, or bent over (dominant gestures by owner).

Because the most common culprit of dominance aggression is a young adult, intact, purebred male, castration is the treatment of choice for individuals fitting this profile. Additional options include behavior modification training, or even Prozac and other drugs, as prescribed by and monitored by a veterinarian.

Controlling Dominance Aggression Against People

Once you know the triggers for your dog's aggressive behavior, take steps to avoid those stimuli. Later, after you've made headway with obedience training and your "no free lunch" program, you can possibly incorporate some of them back into daily concourse with your dog.

Training Tip

The "no free lunch" program means that the dog must earn all the attention, food, play, and toys that he receives from you and other family members. The reward value for these services becomes more valuable when Rover must work for them.

If your dog wants to be petted, ask him to do something like "sit" before you fork over the caress. The coveted contact is now your idea, not his. Limit the amount of and duration of attention. Give him a stroke or two on his chest and then quit. If he wants more, ask him to do something like "fetch" before you resume petting.

The "no free lunch" program does not need to be a long, drawn out process. Dinner, for example, can be a 10 second encounter consisting of giving the command for "sit" followed by your response of "good" when Rover sits, and then placing the food bowl before your dog.

As mentioned in Chapter 4, "Manners Training: Week by Week," avoid wrestling with or playing tug-of-war games with your puppy or dog. Don't allow him to sit on your furniture or sleep in your bed (see Chapter 8, "Housetraining in Every Way"). Go through doors or passage ways before your dog. Refer back to Chapter 9, "Eliminating Annoying Habits," for training tips for the dog that jumps up on people or rushes the door. When you are available to supervise, use a head collar for maintaining additional control of your dog.

Controlling Dominance Aggression Between Dogs

Dogs have a pecking order that serves to maintain peace and to avoid confusion about an individual's place within his social group. In most cases, the resident dog is dominant to a new dog, the older dog is dominant to the younger, the stronger to the weaker, and so on. Later, status might change, and the submissive dog might challenge the dominant one. Dogs demonstrate dominance by growling and standing over those they want to dominate; submissive animals might roll on their back or avert their face from the dominant dog (see Figure 10.1).

> **caution**
> When attempting to restrain your dominant dog, do not place yourself or other family members in peril. Do not use direct confrontations in which you physically try to control your dog by holding his muzzle or using an alpha roll (flipping the dog onto his back and grasping his throat). Avoid punishment devices such as prong or electric shock collars. Call for professional help when you need it.

Often people think in terms of fairness, discouraging displays of dominance within their family of dogs. When you rush in to make sure that the submissive canine has his turn at eating first, being petted first, and other social amenities befitting the higher ranking dog, you are disrupting a system that has worked for eons.

It is better that you acknowledge the dominant dog and show him the favoritism that his status warrants. Give your dogs separate beds, feeding and water bowls, and avoid putting the dogs in situations that might trigger dissention between them.

If aggression is severe, keep the dogs separated and gradually reintroduce them by means of the socialization techniques suggested in Chapter 1, "What You Should Know About Your Dog." Use head collars and leashes as needed to manage encounters.

FIGURE 10.1
A dog exerts his dominance over other dogs in order to have priority access to resources such as toys, food, and attention from the owner.

Preventing Fear Biting

When an animal is afraid, his first choice of action is usually to flee or hide from the perceived threat. When he cannot escape, he will often show ambivalent body language, encompassing fear, submission, and offensive aggression, which might include snarling, growling, and biting.

Dogs prone to fear-related aggression usually display the behavior toward specific people (men, children, veterinarians) or situations (bathing, grooming, and so on). The fear might be because of a genetic predisposition, lack of socialization, or an adverse experience.

Solutions depend on what makes the dog afraid. If you know the trigger, you can take steps to avoid situations that produce fear, or you can reintroduce the fear-inducing person or situation in a non-threatening way. Review Chapter 1 about socialization techniques and making introductions. Teach your children basic bite-prevention techniques (see sidebar).

caution Never break up a dog fight with your bare hands. Distract fighting dogs if possible with water or a citronella spray such as Direct Stop (available at pet stores). Control with collars and leashes.

caution Fear of people, animals, and situations imprints readily in puppies aged 7 to 14 weeks of age. Take special care that introductions to individuals, places, and procedures are positive experiences for your puppy.

CHAPTER 10 Getting Tough About Serious Offenses

BITE PREVENTION DO'S AND DON'TS

* **Do** select a dog with physical and personality traits that fit well with your family.
* **Do** socialize your dog to people, dogs, and other pets.
* **Do** neuter, vaccinate, and license your pet.
* **Do** obedience train your dog.
* **Do** provide your dog with exercise and a stimulating environment.
* **Do** provide your dog with a collar, leash, and ID tags.
* **Don't** leave a baby or small child alone with your dog.
* **Don't** allow your dog to run free or with dog packs.
* **Don't** bother an animal that is sleeping, eating, or caring for babies.
* **Don't** try to take toys or food from an animal.
* **Don't** try to pick up an injured animal. (Call an adult.)
* **Don't** attempt to stop a dog or cat fight. (Call an adult.)
* **Don't** play roughly with your pet.
* **Don't** approach or pet unfamiliar animals.
* **Don't** pursue or fight with a dog that grabs your hat, backpack, or jacket. (Let go and back quietly away.)
* **Don't** run from a dog that chases you (Stop, face the animal without looking directly into his eyes; remain motionless like a tree).
* **Don't** try to out pedal a dog that chases you on your bicycle. (Stop, get off the bike, placing it between you and the dog; back away slowly, using the bike as a barrier between you and the dog.)
* If you are attacked by a dog, drop to the ground and curl into a ball; protect your head and throat by tucking your chin and covering your head with arms and hands.
* **Don't** scream or squeal. (Call for help in as calm a voice as possible.)

Correcting Territorial Aggression

Dogs acting aggressive toward unfamiliar people or animals might be defending what they perceive as their home base or territory. This territory might be the house, yard, boat, or car.

In some cases, the dog perceives that he has successfully chased away the intruder when the UPS employee or meter reader appears to depart in response to the dog's aggressive posturing.

note The Humane Society of the United States reports that small children, the elderly, and letter carriers (in that order) are the most frequent victims of dog bites.

Both sexes are territorial, and neutering has little effect on the behavior. Young adulthood from one to three years seems to be prime time for exhibiting this type of aggression.

Behavioral modification starts with obedience training. The dog should be trained to "sit" and "stay" when strangers appear at the door. Bring aggressive barking under control by teaching the "quiet" command. See Chapter 9 for training suggestions. Use head collars and muzzles (see Figure 10.2) until your dog has proved trustworthy around strangers.

note Visit www.fordogtrainers.com for quality leather or wire muzzles designed for large breed dogs.

note Because approximately one third of all homeowner's claims are dog related, make sure that you are adequately insured. Study local, county, and state ordinances concerning dog ownership.

FIGURE 10.2
A secure, well-fitting muzzle protects others when you and your dog are out in public.

Controlling Predatory Behavior

Predation is a natural extension of the dog's ancestral behavior, designed to stalk, catch, and kill animals for food. Dogs killing rabbits, chickens, sheep, cats, and other animals are indulging in prey behavior. Dogs that chase cars are, in some instances, responding to a predatory instinct.

Domesticated dogs might express predatory behavior in an abbreviated form by chasing and/or catching while not actually following through with the maiming and killing. Others, especially when allowed to run in packs, are dangerous around small animals or children.

CHAPTER 10   **Getting Tough About Serious Offenses**   135

To do list

- [ ] Understand the reasons why your dog chases animals or vehicles
- [ ] Prevent access to people, animals, or vehicles, which trigger predation
- [ ] Review socialization techniques presented in Chapter 1
- [ ] Protect vulnerable people or animals from your dog's predatory behavior
- [ ] Correct your dog when he stalks or chases animals or cars
- [ ] Consult a professional trainer or veterinary behaviorist for assistance with retraining your dog

Things You'll Need

- [ ] Your dog
- [ ] Treats
- [ ] Head collar and leash
- [ ] Containment system such as fence
- [ ] Remote controlled citronella spray collar
- [ ] A car
- [ ] Water balloons

Preventing Predatory Behavior Toward Animals or People

Dogs with a strong predatory drive are enticed into the behavior by cats and other animals that vocalize and run away (see Figure 10.3). In some cases, the dog perceives small children who cry or squeal and run as the same type of prey.

A predatory dog's behavior might include quiet aggression in which no warning is given, or behavioral clues such as staring, agitation, salivating, stalking, circling, slinking, and tail twitching might precede the chase and kill.

Predatory aggression is difficult to control, especially if it has gone on for some time. It is best to avoid the problem in the first place. Socialize your dog to other animals and people; make chase games verboten; increase your dog's

note Although it might be difficult to distinguish from territorial aggression, predatory behavior might explain why some dogs fixate on joggers and bicyclists for aggressiveness.

note Premier Pet Products offers citronella products, including the Spray Commander remote controlled collar. Visit www.premier.com for more information.

exercise; and reinforce obedience commands. Control the dog with a head collar and leash when he is not contained within a fenced yard. Consider using a remote controlled citronella spray collar to distract and punish a dog showing undue interest in passersby.

FIGURE 10.3
A puppy is tempted to chase anything that makes noise and runs.

Train your dog to "stay" when people go by. Enlist a friend to help with training. Wait with your dog while your friend strolls slowly past your yard. Give the dog a command to "sit-stay" and reward him with a favorite treat when he remains quietly at your side. Next time, have your friend step up the pace. Practice over several sessions.

caution I have known many prey-chasing dogs that proved deadly to cats and other pets crossing their paths. Few of these dogs can be rehabilitated. If you can't deny your dog's access to cats and other animals, consult a professional trainer or veterinary behaviorist for assistance with correction. If your dog continues to be a danger to small animals, you should find him a home where he will not be exposed to them. If people are at risk, euthanasia might be the only safe option.

Curbing the Car Chaser

Automobile chasing is dangerous to the dog engaging in it, and often proves distracting to car drivers. This behavior is difficult to change because the dog gets so much enjoyment out of chasing the car away.

One correction technique is to sit in the passenger seat while a family member drives the auto. When the dog takes up the chase, the driver stops the car while you get out and throw water balloons at the dog.

> **tip** You must negatively reinforce the car chasing behavior each and every time it occurs. If the dog chases a car in your absence and has a good time doing it, he is receiving positive reinforcement, which provides incentive to continue the behavior. The best policy is prevention. Deny the dog access to cars by confining him in the house or fenced yard.

To do list

- ❏ Reduce your dog's dependence on you
- ❏ Reinforce the "sit-stay" and "down-stay" commands
- ❏ Use the "no free lunch" method of interacting with your pet
- ❏ Desensitize your dog to the family's departure cues
- ❏ Contact a behavioral consultant or veterinary behaviorist for assistance with behavioral modification techniques

Reducing the Anxiety of Separation

Because domestic dogs consider the human family to be their social group, they become closely bonded to them. For some dogs, separation from one or more of these family members produces extreme anxiety, resulting in problem behaviors such as destruction, barking, inappropriate elimination, and attempts to escape when the beloved owner departs the house.

Things You'll Need

- ❏ Your dog
- ❏ Treats
- ❏ Long-lasting chew toys
- ❏ Comfort Zone with D.A.P. (Dog Appeasing Pheromone) plug-in or spray
- ❏ List of behavioral specialists

Reading the Clues

Dogs diagnosed with separation anxiety are described as overly dependent on or clingy toward one or all human family members. The potential for developing separation anxiety appears to be greater for humane and rescue shelter adoptees than for dogs obtained from individuals. Senior dogs, many of which are sensitive to changes in routine, are more vulnerable to this type of anxiety. Other common background clues include

- Your dog was shielded from separation as a puppy.
- Your dog suffered a traumatic separation experience during the fear-imprinting stage of puppyhood.
- Your dog failed to adjust to your absence when you returned to work after an extended period at home.
- Your dog experienced a stressful event such as a move to a new home or extended period of hospitalization.

Dogs with separation anxiety greet owners with exuberance (jumping, barking, running in circles); avoid being alone, following family members from room to room when they are at home; and appear distressed and anxious when family members prepare to leave the house (see Figure 10.4).

The most disturbing signs of separation anxiety appear when the dog is alone. These include one or more of the following: destruction (often directed toward exits such as doors or windows), excessive vocalizations, house soiling, anorexia and/or vomiting, drooling saliva, and self-mutilation (licking and biting at tails or feet). In most cases, these anxiety-related symptoms occur within 30 minutes of the family's leave taking.

Treating Separation Anxiety

Owners of overly dependent dogs should distance themselves from their pet. This means refusing the dog access to your bedroom at night and the "no free lunch" program discussed earlier in this chapter.

You might inadvertently contribute to your dog's anxiety by communicating concern with extra affection and attention prior to departing and upon returning. Instead, ignore your dog for 15–30 minutes prior to departing the house and when returning. This should be done for all departures and by all family members.

Avoid activities that will stimulate or excite your dog prior to your leaving. If the dog has a room or crate in which he feels secure and safe, send the dog to this area. Provide him with soft music and a long-lasting chew toy such as a Kong filled with peanut butter.

CHAPTER 10 Getting Tough About Serious Offenses 139

FIGURE 10.4
Dogs suffering from separation anxiety are expressing an abnormal fear reaction to being left alone.

Another component to treatment is independence training. Practice "sit-stay" with your dog as you gradually increase your distance from the dog and the duration you expect the dog to hold the "stay" before releasing with "okay." Reward good behavior with a treat. Continue this training until your pet will remain in place up to 30 minutes with the nearest family member in another room.

When these suggestions fail to remedy your dog's anxiety, desensitize to departure cues. Departure cues are the things you do before you leave the house which alert the dog to your impending departure. These include dressing in your suit or uniform, putting on your coat and grabbing your purse or keys, picking up your briefcase or packing the lunch boxes, and turning off the television and lights.

> **note** Comfort Zone with D.A.P. (Dog Appeasing Pheromone) is marketed as a non-prescription product to reduce a dog's stress to new people, situations, and environments. This aerosol is dispersed by plugging into an electrical outlet or by spraying from a bottle. Plug in or spray close to the dog's crate or bed to reduce his anxiety. Visit www.pet-comfortzone.com for information about and uses for their synthetic canine pheromone.

The desensitization process involves giving the departures cues and not leaving the house. You repeat this process until the dog fails to react when you put on your uniform or pack the lunch pails. The next step is to leave the house for tiny increments of time (five minutes to start) in which (hopefully) your dog remains free of anxiety. The length of the departure is slowly increased at five minute intervals.

> **tip** Eliminate departure cues by packing the car the night before or changing into your uniform at work. Mask your departure with distracting noise from the dishwasher or washing machine.

To do list

- ❑ Locate an area within your home or outbuildings to serve as a safe haven for your dog
- ❑ Distract your dog during situations in which he is afraid
- ❑ Desensitize your dog to fear-inducing noise

Reducing Your Dog's Fearful Reactions

A phobia is an intense and irrational fear. Although the phobia can be toward anything, including people, noise is one of the more common triggers. Noise makers engendering fear in some dogs include thunderstorms, fireworks, and gunshots.

If given a choice, most dogs try to escape when they are fearful (flight). Other options are attack (fight), playing possum (freezing), or showing signs of submission. In extreme panic mode, dogs have dug their way under fences and destroyed rooms of homes trying to escape. Because of the potential of injury to the dog and destruction of property, phobias are a serious problem.

> **caution** After-the-fact punishment for destruction or house soiling does not work to change a dog's behavior, and in most cases, serves to increase the dog's anxiety. Desensitization done incorrectly can also serve to worsen problem behavior. Contact a veterinary behaviorist to guide you through the desensitization process. He or she might prescribe anti-anxiety drugs to help facilitate the behavioral modification process.

> **note** Dogs receiving insufficient exposure to a variety of novel places and experiences during the first three months of age are more vulnerable to developing phobias.

Things You'll Need

- ❏ Your dog
- ❏ Food treats
- ❏ Chew toys
- ❏ Interior home space to use as a "panic room"
- ❏ Audio tapes or CDs of phobia-causing sounds
- ❏ Antistatic spray

Calming the Scared Dog

Fear of thunderstorms might be the most common and disruptive of canine phobias. For reasons that are not clear, larger breeds such as Siberian Huskies, Samoyeds, Labrador and Golden Retrievers, and German Shepherds are more frequently affected.

Signs signaling fear in your dog include

- Pacing
- Trembling
- Salivating
- Urinating or defecating
- Attempting to escape
- Vocalizing
- Cowering, crouching, or hiding
- Dilated eyes and laid-back ears

Options for soothing your dog's panic attacks include muting the noise stimuli, providing a sanctuary where your dog can easily escape the fear-inducing situation, distracting, desensitizing, and asking your veterinarian to prescribe anti-anxiety medications.

Closing windows in the house and turning on the television, radio, or stereo might serve to mask fearful sounds. Bring the outside dog into the garage, storage building, or house to help shield him from the noise of storms, fireworks, and gunshots.

In the movie *The Panic Room*, Jodie Foster gave us an awareness of safe havens within our homes. Sometimes, giving a dog a place to go where the sounds of thunder and fireworks are less

> **caution** Avoid forcing the dog into the house, the panic room, or into his crate or kennel, as rough behavior on your part will often make the dog's apprehension worse. Don't use punishment as a correction method.

intense (an interior room or basement) might be helpful. Make sojourns in these "panic rooms" positive for the dog with food treats, soothing music, and toys.

Distraction involves catching the fear-causing situation just as it begins and redirecting the dog's attention. When you anticipate a thunderstorm—the air smells like rain and a few raindrops are falling—give your dog a long-lasting food treat or begin the game of fetch that he enjoys. If the distraction is strong enough and started soon enough, it might be successful in the short term. However, this method is rarely successful in creating lasting change in your dog's phobic behavior.

note Animal Behavior Associates, Inc. offer an hour-long audiotape of thunderstorm sounds (rain, thunder, wind) called *Environments* and various CDs with the sounds of thunderstorms, gunshots, fireworks, and motorized vehicles in their *Sound Sensibilities* series. Peruse their pet owner training products at www.animal-behaviorassociates.com or call (303) 932-9095. Because static electricity might be a component of thunderstorm phobias, consider spraying your dog's bed, crate, and safe sanctuary with antistatic spray.

Desensitization involves gradually exposing the dog to the feared object at a level that does not evoke panic. Subsequent training sessions increase the level of intensity and/or duration of the stimulus. To use this method with noise phobias, increase the noise level of thunder, fireworks, or gunshots in tiny increments using recordings, CDs, or audiotapes. If your dog reacts with fear, you must start over at a previous lesson. It might take 10 brief daily sessions over a period of several months to see positive results.

Summary

In this chapter, you learned that although you cannot change your dog's genetics or past experiences, you can take steps to socialize him to people, other animals, and novel places and situations and to train him to respond to obedience commands.

An understanding of your dog's behavior is a requisite to changing it. I hope that this chapter (and this book) increases your knowledge of why your dog does the things he does and gives you the steps you can take to mold him into a compatible and loving family member.

Part IV

Appendixes

A References and Resources 145

B Planning Charts 153

References and Resources

This appendix provides information about the following:

- Choosing a dog compatible with your family's needs
- Selecting a professional trainer, behavioral consultant, or veterinary behaviorist to assist you with training your dog or correcting his misbehavior
- Websites, telephone numbers, and reference books mentioned in this book

Selecting a Dog

Many factors go into selecting a dog that is a "good fit" for your household. Questions you should ask yourself include what is my home situation, who (pets and people) lives in my home, how much time and money can I devote to my dog, and what role do I expect my dog to fulfill? Once you know the physical and personality canine attributes that best fit your family situation and needs, investigate the breeds offering these traits.

Choosing the Ideal Dog: A Questionnaire

Visit www.Purina.com/Dogs/Behavior for a questionnaire helpful for matching owner needs with compatible dog breeds. Click "Find the Best Dog Breed for You" under the Helpful Links section, and the computer will offer breed recommendations in response to your questionnaire answers. This is similar to a dating service. You enter your profile and needs, and the computer spits out your compatible match or matches. Purina offers information about the 160 breeds in its data banks.

National and local clubs devoted to specific breeds are good resources for information about breeds under consideration. Or borrow a book (Michele Welton's *Your Purebred Puppy: A Buyer's Guide*) from your library.

Accommodating Allergic Family Members

If any of your household members are allergic to dogs, consider the following:

- Give preference to hairless dogs (Chinese Crested and American Hairless Terrier, for example) or breeds with limited shedding potential (Poodle; soft-coated Wheaten Terrier, or Bichon Frise).
- Have the allergic individual spend several hours with the new dog prior to adoption and monitor him for an allergic reaction.
- Make an agreement with the previous owner for a home trial period of two weeks.
- Allergic individuals should wash hands often, sleep in room separate from pet, and limit exposure to pet odors by having another household member clean up after, groom, and feed the dog.
- Brush the dog daily with a soft brush to remove allergy-causing dander and saliva. Wipe the dog weekly with Allerpet (available at pet stores and veterinary clinics) to reduce pet allergens, and bathe pets every two weeks with a mild pet shampoo and cream rinse. Avoid products with strong odors such as doggy perfume or insecticides.

Accommodating Young Children

Humane societies have much experience in facilitating matches between potential owners and abandoned pets. Many recommend that families with children under age 14 avoid adopting dogs showing a predominance of the following breeds: Rottweiler, Pit Bull, Sharpei, Dalmatian, and Cocker Spaniel.

I concur and add a couple of my own—Chow Chow and Akita. You might be surprised that Cockers and Dalmatians made the list. However, they tend to be high-strung and high-energy breeds that mix poorly with small children. Dominance aggression occurs with a fairly high incidence in young adult, purebred male spaniels, especially Cocker and English Springer Spaniels.

APPENDIX A References and Resources

And, yes, I know of exceptions. My favorite granddog was predominantly chow and great with children. I also know sad stories involving some of these breeds and children or other pets. If you are in the choosing stage, it makes sense to avoid a potential problem.

Where to Find a Dog

Once you've narrowed your search to breeds compatible with your family's requirements and your time reserves, give considerable deliberation to where to find your ideal dog.

Considering Humane Society and Rescue Group Dogs

There are benefits to selecting a dog from a humane or animal rescue group. You are giving a needy animal a home; plus, most shelters offer low-cost vaccination and neuter programs. Often, volunteers foster puppies and dogs in individual homes, where they are socialized to people and other animals and taught basic house training and obedience skills. The drawbacks might include exposure to other animals, which increases disease potential, and in some cases, lack of knowledge of the dog's background and ancestry.

You can peruse a listing of dogs available for adoption in shelters in your area (or region, or even across the nation) at www.petfinder.org. This site has 99 breeds in its database with extensive information for each adoptee, including photos, size, age, gender, and available health and background information. Many listings also indicate whether the dog is housebroken or has some obedience training, as well as whether the shelter or rescue group recommends that the dog not share a home with other dogs, cats, or children. Some dogs are listed as requiring special care (dogs testing positive for heartworms, for example).

Considering Pet Store Pups

Many puppies found in pet stores come from puppy mills, which indiscriminately breed dogs and sell puppies. Dogs obtained from pet stores might be stressed from shipment, exposed to diseases, and poorly socialized. Pet store return policies might be a plus for some people.

Considering the Neighbor's Litter

Most pets, especially those falling in the mutt category, are adopted from a friend, neighbor, or individual advertising in the newspaper. Although the genetic background of the litter might be unknown, you should observe the

> **note** Many breed clubs offer rescue groups devoted to abandoned dogs of their representative breed. Volunteers carefully screen dogs up for adoption and potential owners to ensure compatible matches.

mother and, if available, the father in their home environment and ask questions concerning behavior and health care. These questions include

- Is the dam or sire obedience trained?
- Was training easy or difficult?
- Has either dam or sire exhibited behavioral problems such as separation anxiety or aggression toward people or other animals?
- Are the puppies and parents healthy? What type of dog food do they eat?

> **note** Document a complete medical record for the puppy or dog you are adopting to take to your veterinarian. This record should include vaccination history for both dam and puppy—diseases vaccinated against, dates, age at vaccination, person administering the vaccine. Include other pertinent health information—dates of neutering, tests and treatment for external and internal parasites with dates and names of medications used, results of heartworm tests, tattoos or microchips inserted, and any other important medical history.

Puppies often grow up to exhibit the personality traits of their parents. One or the other might act protective of the litter, but extreme aggressive behavior—hair standing on end, bared teeth, and laid-back ears—displayed toward you or the resident human family should be a red light about adopting from this litter. The same goes for homes filled with debris, dirt, and chaos. Home environment is difficult to discern if you've succumbed to the enticement of those cute balls of fur in the Wal-Mart parking lot.

Considering Breeders

Breeders are your primary source for purebred puppies and sometimes adult dogs. They can answer questions about the litter's genetic background; they might monitor and test for specific disease conditions common in their breed; and you can ask to inspect their kennels and observe the condition of their dogs. It is up to you to discern between reputable and disreputable breeders.

The American Kennel Club (AKC), at www.akc.org, posts contacts for breeder referrals as well as links to specific breed clubs, which provide their own breeder referral lists. National and local breed clubs often publish a "Code of Conduct" for breeders. It might state, for example, that responsible breeders will refrain from breeding immature females under age two or that they will complete certain health checks/tests prior to breeding.

Many progressive breeders participate in a database called the Canine Health Information Center (CHIC) located on the Web at www.caninehealthinfo.org. This site gives you information about genetic conditions prevalent in certain breeds, recommendations for disease testing, and a registry of breeders who have tested their dogs for these health conditions.

Selecting a Trainer, Behavioral Consultant, or Veterinary Behaviorist

Selecting the "right" dog trainer or behavioral consultant is an important quest. It can be confusing and difficult because so many people with limited and/or varied qualifications call themselves dog trainers or behavioral consultants. Here are simple descriptions of the most common training professionals:

- **Obedience instructor** teaches you to train your dog.
- **Dog trainer** trains your dog and in turn teaches you how to give the communicating commands.
- **Behavioral consultant** is a person with training and experience in the field of animal behavior. He observes your dog, interprets his behavior, and devises corrective training methods. This person may or may not have master's or doctoral degrees in animal behavior.
- **Veterinary behaviorist** is a veterinarian who is board certified in the specialty of animal behavior. This person has at least two years of post graduate training after veterinary school.

Selecting an Obedience Instructor or Dog Trainer

If you need assistance with obedience training or corrections for misbehaviors, shop around for the most qualified trainer. Ask your veterinarian, the humane society, or members of your breed club.

Check with the National Association of Dog Obedience Instructors at www.nadoi.org for a directory of certified members in your area. These individuals have passed competency tests and demonstrated proficiency in their field. The Certification Council for Pet Dog Trainers at www.ccpdt.org offers a roster of members who have passed certification testing in the field of dog training.

The Applied Companion Animal Behavior Network, at www.acabn.com, offers a directory listing of Approved Dog Trainers—complete with their education, geographical location, websites, and availability of telephone or email consultation services.

caution Anyone can call himself a dog trainer or behaviorist. Therefore, investigate the background, education, experience, training methodology, and certification of the person you select to guide you in training or correcting your dog.

Selecting a Behavioral Consultant or Veterinary Behaviorist

You might need the services of a behavioral consultant for assistance with retraining or correcting long-standing or serious behavioral problems.

In many cases, it is prudent to get someone to come to your house to access your dog's problems in his home environment. If you live in a rural area, a telephone consultation with an experienced behaviorist might set your training or retraining program on the right path. In other instances, you might elect to travel with your dog to a veterinary behaviorist located in a specialty practice or a veterinary school behavioral clinic.

Again, ask someone you trust for a recommendation. Visit the Applied Companion Animal Behavior Network (www.acabn.com) for a directory of approved behavior consultants. Go to the International Association of Animal Behavior Consultants at www.iaabc.org for a directory of members maintaining professional standards or the American College of Veterinary Behaviorists at www.veterinarybehaviorists.org for a listing of veterinarians who are board certified in animal behavior.

Useful Websites, Telephone Numbers, and Books

Included here are websites, telephone numbers, and books mentioned in this appendix or in earlier chapters.

Information

American Kennel Club (**AKC**), www.akc.org—information about 150 dog breeds

American College of Veterinary Behaviorists, www.veterinarybehaviorists.org—directory of veterinarians board certified in animal behavior

Applied Companion Animal Behavior Network, www.acabn.com—directory of approved dog trainers and behavior consultants

Canine Health Information Center, www.caninehealthinfo.org—information about genetic conditions common in dog breeds

Clicker Training, www.clickertraining.com—articles about using clickers for training

Certification Council for Pet Dog Trainers, www.ccpdt.org—directory of certified dog trainers

Dog Patch, www.dogpatch.org/agility—links to articles, equipment, and classes for agility training

APPENDIX A   References and Resources

International Association of Animal Behavior Consultants, www.iaabc.org—directory of certified animal behavior consultants

National Association of Dog Obedience Instructors, www.nadoi.org—directory of certified obedience instructors

Malinut Breed Club, www.malinut.com—animated demonstration of common hand signals used for obedience training

Pet Finders, www.petfinder.org—database of dogs available for adoption from local humane shelters, plus canine body language illustrations

Purina, www.purina.com—questionnaire matching owner profile with compatible dog breeds

Sirius Dog Training, www.siriusdog.com—Volhard Puppy Aptitude Test

U.S. Dog Agility Association, www.usdaa.com, 972-487-2200—site devoted to agility information

Products

Animal Behavior Associates Inc., www.animalbehaviorassociates.com, 303-932-9095—audiotapes/CDs of baby sounds (for socializing dog to babies), storms, and other sounds triggering canine noise phobias

Anti-Icky-Poo, www.mistermax.com, 800-745-1671—enzymatic urine and fecal odor remover

Company of Animals, www.companyofanimals.co.uk—Halti head collar and no-pull harness

For Dog Trainers, www.fordogtrainers.com—dog muzzles

Gentle Leader, www.gentleleader.com, 888-640-8840—head collar and no-pull harness

Handicapped Pets, www.handicappedpets.com, 603-673-8854—bed for pets with urinary incontinence

Invisible Fence, www.invisiblefence.com, 800-578-3647—underground barrier fencing with dog training collar

Kong, www.kongcompany.com, 303-216-2626—chew toys

Lentek, www.lentek.com, 888-353-6835—pet doorbell

Nylabone, www.nylabone.com, 800-631-2188—chew bones

Petapotty, www.petapotty.com, 866-738-7297—sod containment system of potty training

Pet Comfort Zone, www.petcomfortzone.com—synthetic canine pheromone

Pet-2-Ring, www.pet2ring.com—pet doorbell

Premier Pet Products, www.premier.com—citronella spray products

Pupgear, www.doggydocks.com—marine related pet gear

Ruff Doggie, www.ruffdoggie.com—puppy teething toys

Ruff Wear, www.ruffwear.com—dog tent and canine life vest

Scat Mat, www.scatmat.com, 800-767-8658—mat emitting static electricity to keep pets off furniture

Urine-Off, www.urine-off.com—stain and odor remover

Books

Click for Joy: The Clicker Training Answer Book, author Melissa Alexander

Don't Shoot The Dog! The New Art of Teaching and Training, author Karen Pryor

Getting Started: Clicker Training for Dogs, author Karen Pryor

Your Purebred Puppy: A Buyer's Guide, author Michele Walton

B

Planning Charts

This appendix offers charts corresponding to the training lessons presented in Chapter 4, "Manners Training: Week by Week." Use them for quickly ascertaining your training tasks and/or documenting your dog's training progress.

The **Daily Toilet Training Diary** assists you with adhering to a workable potty training schedule and documenting accidents and the circumstances of their occurrence.

The five **Weekly Obedience Training Logs** give you a week by week method of recording your dog's advancement in learning basic obedience commands.

As mentioned earlier, every dog is an individual with different aptitudes for learning tasks such as potty and obedience training. Although verbal communication, potty training, and basic obedience training are presented as a six-week course in Chapter 4, your dog might need longer to become proficient. When he fails to understand a current lesson, regress to and reinforce an exercise your dog knows well. Then, proceed in a series of smaller steps. Your dog might take 12 rather than 6 weeks to become skilled at the tasks presented in Chapter 4.

Daily Toilet Training Diary

In the early stages of toilet training, your dog should go outside at least six to eight times throughout the day and evening. A training "diary" can help you gauge your dog's progress (and pinpoint trouble-prone times or events). Use the following sample to lay out each day of your diary. You can use the symbols "u" for urine and "f" for feces when documenting results of your regularly scheduled potty training sessions and accidents. Accident circumstances might include what family members and your puppy were doing at the time of the accident.

Date: _____

Scheduled Training Time	Result	Accident Time and Location	Accident Circumstances

Weekly Obedience Training Logs

Use the following weekly logs to record progress with obedience training. Remember to keep scheduled training sessions short (less than 15 minutes) and to integrate obedience tasks into daily life with your pet. Use the results column to record responses to various rewards, distractions, and so on.

Weekly Obedience Training Log: "Come" and "Sit" (Introduced Week 2, Chapter 4)

Date	Training Tasks	Training Time	Result
	Come Sit		
	Come Sit		
	Come Sit		
	Come Sit		
	Come Sit		
	Come Sit		
	Come Sit		
	Come Sit		
	Come Sit		
	Come Sit		
	Come Sit		
	Come Sit		
	Come Sit		
	Come Sit		
	Come Sit		

Weekly Obedience Training Log: "Walk" (Introduced Week 3, Chapter 4)

Date	Training Tasks	Training Time	Result
	Come Sit Walk		
	Come Sit Walk		
	Come Sit Walk		
	Come Sit Walk		
	Come Sit Walk		
	Come Sit Walk		
	Come Sit Walk		
	Come Sit Walk		
	Come Sit Walk		
	Come Sit Walk		
	Come Sit Walk		
	Come Sit Walk		

Weekly Obedience Training Log: "Down" (Introduced Week 4, Chapter 4)

Date	Training Tasks	Training Time	Result
	Come Sit Walk Down		
	Come Sit Walk Down		
	Come Sit Walk Down		
	Come Sit Walk Down		
	Come Sit Walk Down		
	Come Sit Walk Down		
	Come Sit Walk Down		
	Come Sit Walk Down		
	Come Sit Walk Down		

Weekly Obedience Training Log: "Sit-Stay" (Introduced Week 5, Chapter 4)

Date	Training Tasks	Training Time	Result
	Come Sit Walk Down Sit-stay		
	Come Sit Walk Down Sit-stay		
	Come Sit Walk Down Sit-stay		
	Come Sit Walk Down Sit-stay		
	Come Sit Walk Down Sit-stay		
	Come Sit Walk Down Sit-stay		
	Come Sit Walk Down Sit-stay		

Weekly Obedience Training Log: "Down-Stay" (Introduced Week 6, Chapter 4)

Date	Training Tasks	Training Time	Result
	Come Sit Walk Down Sit-stay Down-stay		
	Come Sit Walk Down Sit-stay Down-stay		
	Come Sit Walk Down Sit-stay Down-stay		
	Come Sit Walk Down Sit-stay Down-stay		
	Come Sit Walk Down Sit-stay Down-stay		
	Come Sit Walk Down Sit-stay Down-stay		

Index

A

accidents (housebreaking), discouraging, 105
  causes of accidents, 106-107
  excitement-induced urination, 108
  marking behavior, 109
  retraining, 107-108
  submissive urination, 108
activity training, 30. *See also* **exercise; tricks**
adolescent dogs, socializing, 20
age, influence on personality, 11
aggression, 127-128
  dominance-related aggression, 130-131
  fear biting, 132-133
  questions to ask, 129
  territorial aggression, 133-134
agility, 102
AKC (American Kennel Club), 12, 150
allergies to dogs, 146
alpha position, 31
American College of Veterinary Behaviorists, 150
American Kennel Club (AKC), 12, 150
Anderson, Dr. R.K., 19
Animal Behavior Associates, Inc., 142, 151
  Preparing Fido CD, 22
annoying habits. *See* **unwanted behavior, eliminating**
Anti-Icky-Poo, 151
anxiety of separation, 137
  diagnosing, 138
  treating, 138-140
Applied Companion Animal Behavior Network, 150
aptitude for learning, 28
aptitude test (puppies), 14
assessing temperament, 12-14
athletic competitions, 102
attention, getting by clapping, 77
audiotapes, Environments, 142
automobile chasing, 137

B

babies, preparing dogs for, 22-23
backpacking, 96
  doggy packs and supplies, 97
  trail etiquette, 98

bad habits. *See* unwanted behavior, eliminating
bang command, 92
bark collars, 120
barking, excessive, 117-121
begging, 114-115
behavior modification, 107, 130
behavior problems. *See* unwanted behavior, eliminating
behavioral consultants, 149-150
bell ringing trick, 87-89
biting
   bite prevention, 60, 133
   fear biting, 132-133
   puppy biting, 60
body language, 28-29
bow command, 90
bowing trick, 90
Breed Select questionnaire, 146
breeders, 13, 15, 148
breeds
   aptitude for learning, 28
   Breed Select questionnaire, 146
   personality and temperament, 12

C

calming scared dogs, 141-142
Canine Health Information Center, 150
car chasing, 137

cats
   chased by dogs, 136
   introducing dogs to, 25
CDs
   Preparing Fido, 22
   Sound Sensibilities, 142
Certification Council for Pet Dog Trainers, 150
charging clickers, 81
chasing cars, 137
chewing, 60
children
   preparing dogs for, 23
   selecting dogs for, 146-147
choosing
   behavioral consultants, 150
   commands, 50-51
   dog trainers, 149
   dogs, 145-148
   head trainers, 31
   obedience instructors, 149
   veterinary behaviorists, 150
citronella bark collars, 120
clapping to gain dog's attention, 77
clarity of commands, 33-34
classes for puppies, 18
cleaning products, 46
Click for Joy: The Clicker Training Answer Book, 81, 152
clickers, 80
   books/resources, 81
   Clicker Training website, 150
   introducing nail trimming with, 81-83
   loading/charging, 81
   training with, 81
clickertraining.com, 81
collars, 43
   bark collars, 120
   head collars, 76-77
   training dogs to wear, 54
come command
   hand signals, 78-79
   teaching, 57, 72-73
Comfort Zone, 139
commands
   bang, 92
   bow, 90
   choosing, 50-51
   come, 57, 72-73, 78-79
   down, 64-65, 78
   down-stay, 68-69
   drop it, 101
   feedback words, 51
   heel, 74-75, 78
   leave it, 113
   over, 89
   quiet, 119
   release words, 66
   repeated commands, avoiding, 59
   rug, 125
   sit, 57-59, 78
   sit-stay, 66-67
   stay, 66-67, 79
   up, 91
Company of Animals, 151
competitions, 102
conditioning dogs for exercise, 95-96

consistency in training, 33-34
coprophagia (eating feces), 116
correcting misbehavior, 34
corrections, 52
crates
   location of, 39
   size of, 38
   training dogs to use, 51-52
critical periods of social development, 14-15
crotch sniffing, 126

D

D.A.P. (Dog Appeasing Pheromone), 139
daily toilet training diary, 154
den, 38
departure cues, 139-140
desensitization, 120
digging, 112
Direct Stop, 132
Dis-Taste, 116
distractions, 68, 77
Dog Appeasing Pheromone (D.A.P.), 139
dog houses, 40
Dog Patch, 150
dog trainers, 149
doggy packs, 97
dogs, choosing, 145
   allergies to dogs, 146
   breeders, 148
   friend's and neighbor's litters, 147-148
   humane societies/rescue groups, 147

pet stores, 147
Purina Breed Select questionnaire, 146
young children, 146-147
dominance-related aggression
   aggression against people, 130-131
   aggression between dogs, 131
Don't Shoot The Dog! The New Art Of Teaching and Training, 92, 152
door/gate rushing
   doorbell etiquette, 124-125
   preventing, 123-124
doorbell etiquette, 124-125
down command
   down-stay command, 68-69
   hand signals, 78
   teaching, 64-65
down-stay command, 68-69
drinking from toilets, 115
drop it command, 101
drug therapy, 130

E

eating of feces (coprophagia), 116
Environments CD, 142
enzymatic cleaners, 46
equipment
   bark collars, 120
   cleaning products, 46
   collars, 43
   crates, 38-39
   dog houses, 40
   harnesses, 76-77
   head collars, 76-77

ID tags, 43
leashes, 43
toilet training supplies, 40-42
toys, 45-46
treats, 43-44
vendor resources, 151-152
event markers, 80
   books/resources, 81
   introducing nail trimming with, 81-83
   loading/charging, 81
   training with, 81
excessive vocalizations, 117-121
excitement-induced urination, 108
exercise, 93-94
   agility, 102
   athletic competitions, 102
   benefits of, 94
   choosing, 95
   conditioning dogs for, 95-96
   fetch, 101-102
   herding, 102
   hiking and backpacking, 96-98
   hunting, 102
   water sports, 99-100

F

fairness in training, 35
family members
   aggression toward, 130-131
   cooperation during training, 31
   introducing dogs to, 21-23
   predatory behavior toward, 135-136
   socializing older dogs to, 21

How can we make this index more useful? Email us at indexes@quepublishing.com

fearful behavior, 16-18
    calming scared dogs, 141-142
    fear biting, 132-133
    fear-imprinting stage, 16
    noise phobias, 18, 140-142
    separation anxiety, 137-140
feces, eating (coprophagia), 116
feedback
    feedback words, 51
    negative reinforcement, 34
    positive reinforcement, 34
fetch, 101-102
Flight Instinct Period, 20
flotation devices, 100
food, stealing, 112
For Dog Trainers, 151
For-Bid, 116
fordogtrainers.com, 134
free command, 66
fun in training, 35
furniture, keeping dogs off of, 110-111

G

games. *See* **exercise; tricks**
gate/door rushing
    doorbell etiquette, 124-125
    preventing, 123-124
gender, influence on dog's personality, 11
Gentle Leader, 76, 151
***Getting Started: Clicker Training for Dogs*, 81, 152**

go to rug command, 124-125
good (used for praise), 33, 51
grass, urine burn on, 41
greeting behavior of dogs, 24
growling, 118

H

Halti, 76
hand signals, 75
    come command, 78-79
    down command, 78
    heel command, 78
    sit command, 78
    stay command, 79
handicapped pets, 107, 151
harnesses, 43, 76-77
head collars, 43, 76-77
heatstroke, 95
heel command
    hand signals, 78
    teaching, 74-75
    walking on a loose leash, 62-63
hiking, 96
    doggy packs and supplies, 97
    trail etiquette, 98
homeowner insurance claims (dog-related), 134
hoops, jumping through, 91
housebreaking. *See* **toilet training**
howling, 117-121
humane societies, 147
hunting, 102

I

ID tags, 43
immediate feedback, 34
imprinted fears, 16
inside toilet training, 55-56
International Association of Animal Behavior Consultants, 151
introducing dogs to family members/other pets, 21
    babies, 22-23
    cats, 25
    children, 23
    other dogs, 23-24
Invisible Fence, 112, 151

J-K-L

jumping through hoops, 91
jumping up, stopping, 121-122

K-9 Float Coat, 100
Kong, 46, 151

leadership, 31
Leadership Classification Period, 20
leashes, 43
    training dogs to use, 54
    walking on a loose leash, 62-63
leave it command, 113
length of training sessions, 32
Lentek, 151
life jackets, 100
litter boxes, 41

living spaces. *See also* **toilet training**
- crates, 38-39
- dog houses, 40
- furniture, keeping dogs off of, 110-111

loading clickers, 81
location of crates, 39
locations for training, 31-32

M

mailmen, 16
Malinut website, 151
manners training, 30, 49-50. *See also* **toilet training; unwanted behavior, eliminating**
- clickers, 80-83
- collar and leash training, 54
- come command, 57, 72-73, 78-79
- commands, choosing, 50-51
- crate training, 51-52
- definition of, 30
- distractions, 68
- dog's attention, getting by clapping, 77
- down command, 64-65, 78
- down-stay command, 68-69
- feedback words, 51
- hand signals, 75-79
- heel command, 74-75, 78
- leave it command, 113
- patience, 69
- puppy biting, 60
- puppy chewing, 60

release words, 66
repeated commands, avoiding, 59
required equipment and supplies, 50
sit command, 57-59, 78
stay command, 66-67, 79
walking on a loose leash, 62-63

marking behavior (toilet training), 109
matching dogs with training techniques, 28-29
misbehavior. *See* **unwanted behavior, eliminating**
moaning, 118
mounting, 126
Mutt Hutt tents, 97
muzzles, 134

N

nail trimming, 81-83
naming dogs, 33
National Association of Dog Obedience Instructors, 151
negative reinforcement, 34
neutering, 11
nicknames, 33
nipping (puppies), 60
"no free lunch" program, 130-131
no-pull harnesses, 76-77
no (used for correction), 21, 33, 51, 61
noise phobias, 18
nose-to-crotch sniffing, 126
Nylabone, 46, 151

O

obedience instructors, 149
obedience training, 30, 49-50. *See also* **toilet training; unwanted behavior, eliminating**
- clickers, 80-83
- collar and leash training, 54
- come command, 57, 72-73, 78-79
- commands, choosing, 50-51
- crate training, 51-52
- definition of, 30
- distractions, 68
- dog's attention, getting by clapping, 77
- down command, 64-65, 78
- down-stay command, 68-69
- feedback words, 51
- hand signals, 75-79
- heel command, 74-75, 78
- leave it command, 113
- patience, 69
- puppy biting, 60
- puppy chewing, 60
- quiet command, 119
- release words, 66
- repeated commands, avoiding, 59
- required equipment and supplies, 50
- sit command, 57-59, 78
- sit-stay command, 66-67
- stay command, 66-67, 79
- walking on a loose leash, 62-63

okay command, 66

older dogs, socializing
    to other dogs, 20-21
    to other people, 21
outside toilet training, 40-41, 54
over command, 89
overheating, 95

P

packs (backpacking), 97
paper training, 40-41
patience, 69
patience in training, 35
people
    aggression toward, 130-131
    cooperation during training, 31
    introducing dogs to, 21-23
    predatory behavior toward, 135-136
    socializing older dogs to, 21
personality of dogs
    assessing, 12-14
    body language, 28-29
    influences on, 9-12
    matching dogs with training techniques, 28-29
Pet Chime, 88
Pet Comfort Zone, 152
pet stores, 147
Pet-2-Ring Doorbell, 88, 152
PetaPotty, 41-42, 151
petcomfortzone.com, 139
Pet Finder, 151

phobias. *See* **fearful behavior**
planning charts, 153
playing dead, 92
positive reinforcement, 34, 43-44
postmistress, 119
potty accidents, discouraging, 105
    causes of accidents, 106-107
    excitement-induced urination, 108
    marking behavior, 109
    retraining, 107-108
    submissive urination, 108
potty training. *See* **toilet training**
predatory behavior, 134
    car chasing, 137
    toward animals/people, 25, 135-136
Premier Pet Products, 135, 151
Preparing Fido CD, 22
primary rewards, 52
problem behaviors. *See* **unwanted behavior, eliminating**
proofing of training lessons, 68
Prozac, 130
punishment, 34, 52, 111
PupGear, 100, 152
puppies
    biting behavior, 60
    chewing, 60

    crate training, 51-52
    personality, 9-12
    Puppy Aptitude Test, 14
    socialization, 15-19
    temperament testing, 13-14
    toilet training, 53-56
Puppy Aptitude Test, 14
Purina, 151
    Second Nature litter box system, 41
    Breed Select questionnaire, 146
pushy behavior at doors/gates
    doorbell etiquette, 124-125
    preventing, 123-124

Q-R

recall. *See* **come command**
recreational activities. *See* **exercise; tricks**
reinforcement
    negative reinforcement, 34
    positive reinforcement, 34, 43-44
release words, 66
remote punishment, 111
repeated commands, avoiding, 59
rescue groups, 147
retraining (toilet training), 107-108
retrieving toys, 101-102
rewards, 52
rolling over on command, 89

Ruff Doggie, 152
Ruff Wear, 100, 152
rug command, 125
rules of training
  clarity and consistency, 33-34
  fairness, 35
  fun, 35
  immediate feedback, 34
  negative reinforcement, 34
  patience, 35
  positive reinforcement, 34

S

Scat Mat, 111, 152
scheduling training sessions, 32-33
Second Nature litter box system, 41
secondary rewards, 52
selecting
  behavioral consultants, 150
  dog trainers, 149
  obedience instructors, 149
  veterinary behaviorists, 150
separation anxiety, 137
  diagnosing, 138
  treating, 138-140
shaping, 92
shock bark collars, 120
sign language. *See* **hand signals**
Sirius Dog Training, 151

sit command, 57-59, 78
sit-stay command, 66-67
SleePee Time Bed, 107
slip collars, 43
sniffing crotch area, 126
socialization
  adolescent dogs, 20
  critical periods of development, 14-15
  older dogs, 20-21
  puppies, 15-19
sod boxes, 41-42
sod training, 41-42
sonic bark collars, 120
sports. *See* **exercise**
stay command, 66-67, 79
stealing toys/food, 112
submissive urination, 108
sunburn, 95
sunscreen, 95
swimming, 99-100

T

temperament
  assessing, 12-14
  body language, 28-29
  influences on, 9-12
  matching dogs with training techniques, 28-29
territorial aggression, 133-134
timing of reinforcement, 34

toilet training, 53
  causes of accidents, 106-107
  cleaning products, 46
  excitement-induced urination, 108
  how long it takes, 56
  inside, 55-56
  litter boxes, 41
  marking behavior, 109
  outside, 40-41, 54
  paper, 40-41
  retraining, 107-108
  sample schedule for working owners, 53
  submissive urination, 108
  toilet training diary, 154
toilets, drinking from, 115
toys
  choosing, 45-46
  dogs stealing toys, 112
trail etiquette, 98
training lesson charts, 153
training logs, 155-159
treats, 43-44
tricks, 85-86
  bell ringing, 87-89
  benefits of trick training, 86
  bowing, 90
  choosing, 86-87
  jumping through hoops, 91
  playing dead, 92
  rolling over, 89
trimming nails, 81-83

How can we make this index more useful? Email us at indexes@quepublishing.com

U

U.S. Dog Agility Association, 151
ultrasonic bark collars, 120
unwanted behavior, eliminating
  barking and excessive vocalizations, 117-121
  begging, 114-115
  biting, 60, 132-133
  coprophagia (eating feces), 116
  digging, 112
  dominance-related aggression, 130-131
  fear and phobias, 132-133, 140-142
  furniture, keeping dogs off of, 110-111
  jumping up, 121-122
  mounting, 126
  nose-to-crotch sniffing, 126
  predatory behavior, 134-137
  pushy behavior at doors/gates, 123-125
  separation anxiety, 137-140
  stealing toys/food, 112
  territorial aggression, 133-134
  toilet drinking, 115
up command, 91
urine burn on grass, 41
Urine-Off, 46, 152

V-Z

verbal commands, 50-51. *See also specific command names*
veterinarians, first visits to, 17-18
veterinary behaviorists, 149-150
Volhard, Jack and Wendy, 14

walking on a loose leash, 62-63
water sports, 99-100
weekly obedience training logs, 155-159
when to train, 32-33
where to train, 31-32
whimpering, 118
whining, 117-121

yelping, 118
Your Purebred Puppy: A Buyer's Guide, 152

Training Notes

Training Notes

Training Notes

Training Notes

Training Notes

Training Notes

Training Notes

Training Notes

Training Notes

Training Notes

Training Notes

Training Notes